DELEGATE

DOUBLE THE RESULTS!
HALVE THE EFFORT!

SALLY FOLEY-LEWIS

ISBN 978-0-9874186-6-1

Cover design and layout: Lauren Shay - Full Stop Writing, Editing, and Design.

Images: Sally Foley-Lewis

Internal design: Olivier Darbonville

ABOUT THE AUTHOR

Sally Foley-Lewis

Sally Foley-Lewis has spent the past 20 years helping people to become better leaders and be more productive. She develops leaders' efficiency by building their people and team skills, improving their task management, and nurturing their self-leadership. She works with middle managers and team leaders in large corporates and associations in Australia and overseas, as well as owners of medium-sized businesses.

Essentially, she is a productivity and leadership expert.

Obsessed with execution, Sally enables people to get on with their work and get along with their peers, senior leaders, and teams. The flow-on effect of this is profound: leaders witness an even greater level of engagement and productivity from their team members.

What makes Sally different from other leadership experts is that she has both functioned as manager and CEO. She knows first-hand the pressure of balancing your own workload, leading a team, and delivering the required outcomes. Sally has experienced the struggle of life in the trenches, so she truly gets it!

Sally has also trained and developed managers and leaders across a diverse range of industries in Australia and overseas. Her unique skill set and depth of experience means she knows how to make real, lasting improvements to productivity, leadership and performance.

As a leader, working with different people means managing, influencing and maneuvering different personalities. You may be avoiding delegating tasks that deep down you know you should, but you're unsure how to start or whom to ask, as the outcome is unknown. There is a risk and this may make you uncomfortable or unsure where to start. So you are left with more work than time available and possibly starting your own work when everyone else has left for the day. This makes achieving what's required tougher than it should be.

Sally understands this. She can help you understand, plan and implement a structure so you can begin the delegation conversations you need to have with confidence. So you can move forward. She can help you work through your fears, take control of your leadership, and be excited about your work and your team's work.

Sally speaks, mentors, trains, and coaches individuals and teams in the areas of delegation, feedback, productivity, and self-leadership. She does this through workshops, presentations, and mentoring for leaders who want to build their skills and confidence so they can lead their teams more effectively – by delegating appropriately, leading difficult conversations with confidence, and giving feedback in ways that affect positive change.

To find out more about Sally and her programs, go to
www.sallyfoleylewis.com.

ACKNOWLEDGEMENTS

It might seem over the top to some that I believe so deeply in the leadership and development value of delegating. I'll be the first to admit I'm a tad bit obsessed with delegating. My own experiences have reinforced its value and, like many lessons in life, once we make a few mistakes the learning tends to be more powerful so our life, and our skills make the way forward more effective and productive.

Like any other book that is written, the author is only one member of the team that creates the final product. The author is one part of a process.

To Lyndal Hansen, whose leadership has been an example for me for more than 20 years. Lyndal was my first ever boss to show how delegating could be done and get results, with what seemed like an effortless balance between support and supervision.

To my mentors also, who have invited me to step up and play a bigger game, without your push, provocation and passion I wouldn't be writing this, let alone my previous books. I want to acknowledge Thought Leaders Business School, in particular Jane Anderson and Col Fink.

To the clients I work with every day, your positive impact on your team is an inspiration and it's an honor to be in your world.

To Martin, who constantly shows me the value of deep thinking and demonstrates his love and devotion through patience and deed. Thank you. Thank you for being you and encouraging me to be my best. I love you.

CONTENTS

PART 3 - HOW TO DELEGATE

INTRODUCTION

At the start of a short-term internship project in 1999, the manager handed over a thick report and said, "Read this, then let's talk about how you will fix it."

That moment, I later realised, was a tipping point for me as an employee, project manager, and future leader; and how empowering the skill of delegating can be for manager and employee both, when it's done well. The manager set me up for success in the project, not an easy project by any means, but she knew what she was doing even if I didn't yet. She stated that she trusted me, that she wasn't going to micromanage or hover so if I had questions by all means ask but it was me who had the authority to achieve the desired outcome. She stepped in when I asked and she facilitated, rather than directed. When I needed her level of authority, which was really only a signature here or a nod there, I wasn't kept waiting. We scheduled milestones and meetings so that she could be kept up to date and provide whatever support I needed.

That experience has stayed with me ever since. I was trusted and supported; I was empowered and given the right level of authority and responsibility that matched the project to my abilities. My confidence grew alongside my skills and I am convinced that was a significant contributor to securing a full-time position with the organisation.

But as the zen wisdom from Lao Tzu states, "To know and not do is to not yet know" would sum up my first experience of leading in a workplace. In hindsight, the excitement of being in a new role, blended in with wanting to be helpful, meant I inadvertently stepped on toes and was performing tasks that really should have been done by other employees. Once I was made aware of what I was doing, it sunk in that I was not being effective in my role and making others roles a challenge. Having an open, respectful and trusting relationship meant this could be rectified quickly and easily.

Now I've got it!

Over the years, working with thousands of managers and leaders across the world, their experiences of, skills in, and perceptions held about delegating vary widely. However what does not vary is their desire to do well. Watching a manager transform from being resistant to delegating, to learning and embracing the key steps, and then applying them with success is an honour and I do love it when I hear, "Why haven't I been delegating sooner?"

DELEGATE - Double the Results! Halve the Effort! is in three main parts.

Part one will give you insights into why delegation is an essential skill for every manager. From years of working with managers and management teams, I've compiled a list of reasons why delegation is so hard: you might recognise some from your own experience. Once you can identify your roadblocks - truly name them and get them out in the open, as such - you can then work on the right skills and elements to make delegation a dream. A quick look at how delegation fits into leadership, culture and generations will also help set the scene in a broader context for being a successful delegator.

Part two is the foundation for your delegating success: the right skills, strategies and mindset are what make delegating work for you rather than against you. While you might be tempted to go straight to part three for the steps, skipping this part will make implementing the steps that much harder. The secret to delegating successfully lies in part two!

It's a bit like being a house painter: you have to clean the wall, maybe remove wallpaper or old paint, remove old picture hooks, fill those holes, sand, and undercoat .... You'll do all this before actually painting the wall with your chosen colour! If you want a lovely painted wall, then you have to prepare the surface. That's what part two is all about, preparing the surface.

It's critical to cover in detail the core success factors to ensure the whole process of delegating will work and not blow up in your face: including relationships and trust, and understanding the distinction between responsibility and authority.

Part three gets down to business! How to delegate: all laid out in nine steps. Each of the nine steps will be pulled apart so that when you next come to delegate you are more discerning, strategic, and confident and you end up with a more developed and engaged team. They are happier, you are happier!

Take your time with this book. Keep it handy and use it as a reference guide. I dream of walking into your office one day and seeing your copy of DELEGATE sitting on your desk well worn because it has served you well. That is my goal for writing this book, to serve you well.

You'll find links to downloadable templates and resources are included. If you have any questions, feedback or would like a delegation workshop for your team, I'd love to hear from you. You can contact me at *sally@sallyfoleylewis.com.*

Delegation is
NOT a dirty word.

SALLY FOLEY-LEWIS

PART ONE

WHY DELEGATE

CHAPTER 1

WHAT IS DELEGATION?

Delegate[1] - *verb*

- To entrust another
- To appoint as one's representative
- To assign responsibility or authority

First known use of the word delegate: Verb – it is used 1530 times in the meaning of entrusting another.

Middle English ***delegat***, from Medieval Latin ***delegatus***, from Latin, past participle of ***delegare*** to delegate, from ***de-*** + ***legare*** to send.

Enough of the English lesson, let's look at delegation as it applies to you now, today…

With the ever increasing demand to get more done, in seemingly less time and without extra resources, delegation needs to be a key skill for any successful manager. Delegating is, in simple terms, allocating tasks, or roles to another. A simple definition yet its execution can be a significant challenge for some managers providing a real block to success.

---

[1] https://www.merriam-webster.com/dictionary/delegating#h2

It's when you identify and eliminate key blockages to delegating, and work through each of the steps to delegating properly you gain the real value this essential managerial skill offers. There's really no quick fix, magic wand, silver bullet way to delegating with full confidence and structure if you are starting out with concerns of trust; a lack of clarity of the standards and expectations you want; not sure what to actually delegate; why you should delegate.

Stephen R. Covey, the author of the famous book *The 7 Habits of Highly Effective People*, said,

Efficiency with people is ineffective. With people, fast is slow and slow is fast.

With delegating slow is most definitely fast. But don't despair, when you've got the nine steps embedded fully in your tool kit you'll soon see how productive and engaged you and your team will be. Do the set up properly at the front end of the delegation so that when the work starts it happens quickly and smoothly, with significantly less risk of errors, issues, stoppages; and far greater chances of success and confidence.

This book is your how-to for delegating. The aim is to provide you the essential insights, practical guidance, and templates so you can start delegating or make delegating easier for you. After all, isn't easier what we all want?

Delegating is a skill and a strategy to get work done effectively and efficiently. The right people, using the right skills, doing the right work. Delegation can be the simple discharge of a task or project or a cost effective and exciting development opportunity.

I don't keep a dog and bark myself.

ELIZABETH I

CHAPTER 2

LEADERSHIP AND DELEGATION

British statistician, George Box, is credited with saying, "all models are wrong, but some are useful". This is helpful to keep in mind when reviewing and determining if you'd follow a leadership model. No model or leadership theory can include all the variables that would make the role of delegating, let alone managing, confident and complete.

Like shopping, you have your favourite brands for some staple items and you'll rely on being able to buy them regularly, simply because they work for you or they fit your style or tastes. Then you'll see some specials in the middle of an aisle, or you see a product promotions person enticing you to taste the new product they are spruiking and so you think, "Ooh, I'll try a bit of that!" or "It's on special, so I'll try it at this special price."

Models and theories are like shopping, some you'll like and some you won't. Pablo Picasso has been attributed saying, "Learn the rules like a pro, so you can break them like an artist". This holds true for leadership theories.

From the plentitude of leadership theories and models devised over the decades, here is a cursory view of only a few, viewed through the lens of delegation:

Situational Leadership II Theory[2] - Dr. Paul Hersey and Kenneth Blanchard

This is a framework to help identify and match the style of leadership to the situation at hand.

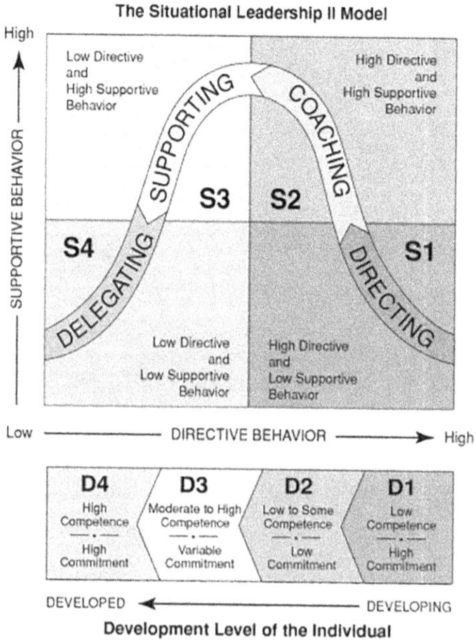

Delegating is seen as being most appropriate when supportive behaviour and directive behaviour requirements are both low. In other

---

[2] https://www.kenblanchard.com/Products-Services/Situational-Leadership-II and image source: https://sk.sagepub.com/books/developing-human-service-leaders/i697.xml

words, the employee (delegate) has a high level of competence and a high level of commitment.

While this may be one of the most popular leadership models and limits delegating to only those who are highly willing and highly skilled, delegating has the potential to develop as you'll discover in part three of this book.

Aligning an employee's level of development to the leadership style or approach required is helpful.

Tannenbaum-Schmidt Leadership Continuum[3] - Robert Tannenbaum and Warren Schmidt

This model embraces the notion that there is no one style of leading that works for every given situation. This leadership continuum looks at the link between the authority of the leader and the freedom it provides the team/employee. This model considers three factors when determining a style to use, the:

1. Individual leaders preferred style and value,
2. Team, and the leader's relationship with the team, and the team's readiness for responsibility, and
3. Situation and the level of importance of the work, deadlines and the organisation's culture.

Progression through the styles in this model hinges on who decides, even at the Delegates level. The manager still defines the limits prior to the

---

[3] https://expertprogrammanagement.com/2018/11/tannenbaum-schmidt-leadership-continuum/. Images source: https://www.researchgate.net/figure/Continuum-of-leadership-behaviour-Tannenbaum-Schmidt-1973-exhibit-1-p4_fig1_323736322

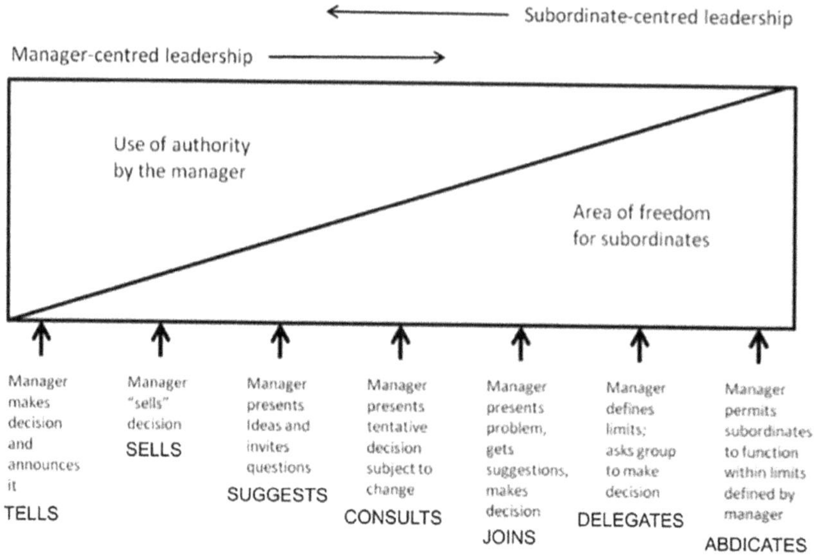

delegate's decision. While managers do need to translate the strategic plan, the vision of the business, into operational and action plans, the successful manager will involve key team members, if not the whole team in defining the limits, boundaries and opportunities. By doing this, it will increase engagement.

The final level of Abdicates gives a false impression that the manager is completely hands-off. This is not realistic. The diagonal line inside the model that shows the increasing level of subordinate centered leadership and decreasing manager centered leadership could be more accurate if there's a small amount of manager-centered leadership maintained at the Abdicated level, such as:

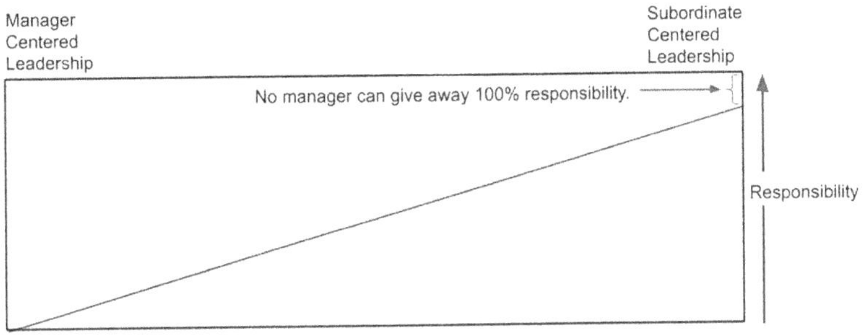

As the manager of your team, you simply can not give away all the responsibility entrusted in your role and your level of authority. When delegating, you do hand over authority and responsibility pertaining to the task or project but you will always have ultimate responsibility.

Levels of Delegation Models

A Google search of the phrase *levels of delegation* will offer you more than 44.6 million results! Interestingly many of these results are presented as memes and the attribution of authorship is missing or difficult to discern accurately.

Some of these models are not strictly levels of delegation but rather levels of management or leadership that include, amongst other elements of leading, deciding, engaging, task allocation, and delegating. There's a similarity amongst many of these models to the Tannenbaum-Schmidt Leadership Continuum.

These levels of delegation are like memes that are popular and provide a simple structure to guide delegation. Aid de memoires are incredibly useful to have on hand only after you know what you're doing. Take these two examples:

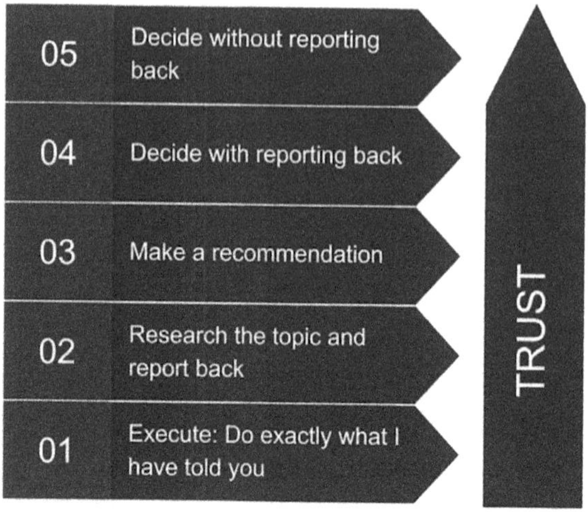

As cited in a blog post by Michael Hyatt[4]:

I DO	Realisation
I DO, YOU WATCH	Observation
WE DO	Collaboration
YOU DO, I WATCH	Evaluation
YOU DO	Delegation

What these models lack is depth in indicating when to use which level, and assumes a certain level of self-awareness, skills mastery and discernment to match level to task and to employee (delegate).

---

[4] https://michaelhyatt.com/the-five-levels-of-delegation/
More on theories of leadership can be found at: http://www.changeminds.org/disciplines/leadership/theories/leadership_theories.htm

In the first example, you might assume that you need greater trust as you move up the levels, or your trust in the delegate increases as you move toward level five. I contend that your success as a manager needs trust as a core foundation with all your team members no matter if you're considering delegating to some or coaching or training others. With trust comes confidence: you trust your team and are confident in their ability to do the work and your team trusts you and their confidence improves through stepping up into more or more challenging work through delegating. Furthermore, if a task is completely new and the employee is at level one - *Execute* - from the first example, and *I DO* in the second example – trust is not the focus, it needs to be knowledge transfer and skills acquisition.

Start with relationship and trust building so that, even at the lowest level, where skill maybe lacking, the strength of the relationship ensures a smoother and faster journey to skills mastery and easier delegating.

It is possible to fly without motors, but not without knowledge and skills.

WILBUR WRIGHT

INVENTOR OF WORLD'S FIRST SUCCESSFUL AIRPLANE

CHAPTER 3

CULTURE AND DELEGATION

From living and working in Germany, the United Arab Emirates, and Australia and traveling internationally delivering hundreds of management skills training sessions for middle managers it's always interesting to observe and hear such diverse thinking and approaches to delegating. Some would be extremely hesitant to delegate while others would be at the other extreme (almost exploiting it), and others plotted along all points in between. What all this has taught me is:

- everyone wants to do well,
- everyone has their own unique way, style, approach to delegating, and
- cultural background has an influence on how one delegates and on how one accepts delegation.

Any country that has significant cultural diversity, like Australia, needs its leaders and managers to consider the cultural background of their team members when planning delegation. Even with some minor insight into the culture, a manager can adjust their communication and approach in order to make delegating successful.

Professor Geert Hofstede[5], whose exceptional cultural work is based on six cultural dimensions, can help you quickly understand the differences between cultures. The six dimensions are:

1. *Power Distance:* measures the view of power in relationships.
2. *Individualism (or Collectivism):* is the emphasis on individual or group.
3. *Masculinity:* the level or degree of expectations for men and women.
4. *Uncertainty Avoidance:* the measure of comfort with stability, structured rules and risk.
5. *Long Term Orientation:* whether the focus is on forgoing short-term gratification for long term gain; level of focus on preparing for the future.
6. *Indulgence (or Restraint):* extent to which people control their desires and impulses, fun or restraint and follow strict social norms.

While all six dimensions are valuable to understand, if you simply compared cultures across power distance, individualism and uncertainty avoidance, as influencers of success or otherwise for delegating, as shown in table 1.1, it's easy to see that taking the time to understand your people, including cultural influences, will improve your delegating results. According to the Australian Bureau of Statistics[6], the largest nationalities by population in Australia are Australian, British (UK), New Zealand, Chinese, Indian and Malaysian. I've added some more cultures in table 1.1 to demonstrate the diversity and highlight the need to adapt your delegation approach.

---

[5] https://www.hofstede-insights.com/country-comparison/

[6] https://www.abs.gov.au/ausstats/abs@.nsf/Lookup/by%20Subject/2071.0~2016~Main%20Features~Cultural%20Diversity%20Data%20Summary~30

Table 1.1: Cursory comparison of cultural differences

COUNTRY	POWER DISTANCE	INDIVIDUALISM	UNCERTAINTY AVOIDANCE
Australia	38	90	51
United Kingdom	35	89	35
New Zealand	22	79	49
China	80	20	30
India	77	48	40
Malaysia	100	26	36
Philippines	94	32	44
Germany	35	67	65
UAE	90	25	80
USA	35	91	35

Cultural competency is an absolute advantage for any manager leading and delegating. These insights can be helpful, yet remember that not even two Australians are exactly alike. The following provides a generalised example of how delegating across cultures may need to focus more heavily on some steps than others:

With a high power distance culture: e.g. Malaysia: subordinates expect to be told what to do and challenging management is not well received. A direct report with this cultural background might expect more direction, at least initially in setting up the delegation. Ideas are less likely to be challenged, which means if the idea (task or project) is not well thought out, the wrong idea might be executed.

With a low power distance culture: e.g. Australia: managers and employees enjoy shared consultation and information dissemination; communication is informal, direct and participative. Delegation based on an egalitarian approach would work well.

With a high individualism culture: e.g. USA: one of the most individualist cultures in the world, where managers rely on employees and teams for their expertise. Employees and managers expect to be consulted in environments where communication is direct and informal. Delegating that invites input into the planning of the task or project would work well.

With a low individualism (collective) culture: e.g. China: employee commitment to the organisation is low whereas people will act in the interest of a group, especially an in-group (e.g. family). Personal relationships hold more power over tasks therefore delegating has a higher potential for success when there is a strong relationship in place.

With a high uncertainty avoidance culture: e.g. United Arab Emirates: There is a high reliance and need for rules and rigid codes of belief. Innovation may be resisted if security and precision are challenged. Delegating successfully relies on creating boundaries, a sense of safety (reduced risk) and precision.

With a low uncertainty avoidance culture: e.g. India: Nothing has to go exactly as planned, nothing is perfect, there's a high tolerance for the unexpected. There's a tendency to settle into established roles and routines and rules are to be circumvented: one adjusts as a way to work out a problem. Delegating could lead to some innovative and creative outcomes, so long as the rules that must not be broken are explicitly known.

SELF-COACHING QUESTIONS

Go to https://www.hofstede-insights.com/country-comparison/

1. What is your cultural background? How do you relate and differ from the information in Table 1.1 or online?

2. What is the cultural background of your team members?

3. Thinking about two or three people you are keen to delegate to, what are their cultural backgrounds?

4. Go to https://www.hofstede-insights.com/country-comparison/ and search the different cultures: what insights does this give you about how to lead and delegate?

*When I put out to sea,
I do not offer advice
to the skipper about
the management of
the ship.*

ELSA BARKER
AMERICAN NOVELIST

CHAPTER 4

DELEGATION ACROSS GENERATIONS

Inside an organisation, you might see four or five generations working alongside each other. This can provide some interesting challenges for managing, leading and delegating. A Baby Boomer (1946-1964) being managed by a Gen Y (1981 to 2000) is not uncommon now. For it to be successful it only needs a little thinking and some planning that takes generational differences into account. Like cultural differences, these are generalisations that help give context, but it's important to remember that no two people from the same generation are exactly the same. In table 1.2 are some insights into the different generations that provide a good starting point to learn further about each person.

GENERATIONAL DIFFERENCES*

Generation	Traditional / Veteran	Baby Boomers	Gen X	Gen Y / Millennial	Gen Z / iGen
Year	1900-1945	1946-1964	1965-1980	1981-2000	1996-
Influenced by	▪ War ▪ Great Depression ▪ Space Race	▪ Vietnam War ▪ Cold War ▪ High divorce rates ▪ The Contraceptive Pill ▪ Yuppies	▪ Watergate ▪ Latchkey Kids ▪ Y2K ▪ Downsizing	▪ Digital ▪ AIDS ▪ 9/11 ▪ Social conscious to fix parents and grandparents mistakes ▪ Busy kids	▪ Environment ▪ Disruption ▪ Unicorns ▪ Social Media ▪ Tech native Throwback: blend of technology of today and elements of past generations
Values	▪ Rules ▪ Discipline ▪ Don't question authority ▪ Hard work ▪ Giving back	▪ Equal rights ▪ Equal opportunities ▪ Anti war ▪ Anti government ▪ Personal Gratification	▪ Diversity ▪ Highly educated ▪ Independent ▪ Balance ▪ Entrepreneurial ▪ High job expectations	▪ Global ▪ Civic ▪ Personal attention ▪ Social ▪ Self-confident ▪ Technically proficient and agile	▪ Environment ▪ Life will be what I make it ▪ Less concerned with security and privacy
Authority	Seniority and tenure	Longevity leads to loyalty	Sceptical of authority and will test repeatedly	Will test and also seek guidance	▪ Freelance ▪ Influencer
Focus	Task	Relationships and Results	Task and Results	Global and Networked	▪ Financial rewards ▪ Self-reliant and long-term contribution to the economy

Advancement	Seniority	Experience	Merit	Contribution	Collaboration
Work environment	▪ Hierarchical ▪ Top-down management	▪ Democratic ▪ Flat hierarchy	▪ Fast paced ▪ Informal ▪ Fun and functional	▪ Creative ▪ Diverse ▪ Collaborative ▪ Feedback	▪ Fun workplace ▪ Flexible work schedule ▪ Collaborative
How authority is viewed	Respected	Impressed	Unimpressed	Relaxed	Relaxed
Style	Individual	Team Player so meetings are common	Entrepreneur	Participative	Flexible
Motivate me	▪ Respect my experience ▪ Security	▪ I am valued and needed ▪ Money	▪ Let me do it my way Rules come second ▪ Freedom and time off	▪ Surround me with creative people ▪ Bright people ▪ Time off	▪ Variety ▪ Creative people ▪ Paid time off
Delegation Style	▪ Directive ▪ Ask what's worked before ▪ Value their stability and sense of community ▪ Determine standards and rules together	▪ Collegial ▪ Emphasise the importance of their role ▪ Check in but avoid micromanaging ▪ Show how status will be positively affected	▪ Competence driven so will challenge and ask why ▪ Allow flexibility ▪ Encourage creativity ▪ Listen and help them take responsibility by appreciating how their work affects the organisation	▪ Achievement driven ▪ Set goals together ▪ Set a plan specifically with and for them ▪ Acknowledge their decisions	▪ Fellowship and continual dialogue ▪ Recognition and advancement opportunities ▪ Link to new technologies ▪ Prepare them with relevant skills

Table 1.2: Summary of generational differences

***NOTES**

1. This is a comprehensive chart of differences worth exploring: http://www.wmfc.org/uploads/GenerationalDifferencesChart.pdf
2. https://genhq.com/faq-info-about-generations/
3. https://staffbase.com/blog/generation-z-in-the-workplace-5-ways-to-be-a-better-employer/
4. https://www.researchgate.net/publication/265237327_Generational_Differences_Impact_On_Leadership_Style_And_Organizational_Success

---

As you can see from this summary of generations, the level of communication, reassurance, planning and supporting can be adapted to suit the generation of the delegate. This is a guide only, it cannot replace quality time and effort spent getting to know the individual.

SELF-COACHING QUESTIONS

1. What generation category do you fit into? Reading your category in Table 1.2, do you agree with the descriptions? How do you relate and differ?

2. Which generations make up your team?

3. Thinking about one person who fits into a different generation to you: what insights from Table 1.2 do you now have, combined with your current understanding of the person - their work style and communication style - that will affect the way you delegate?

You are nothing, nothing, without a good team. It's important to surround yourself with people whose opinion you trust.

DAME ANNA WINTOUR DBE

BRITISH-AMERICAN JOURNALIST AND EDITOR OF VOGUE

CHAPTER 5

WHY DELEGATING IS HARD TO DO?

Over the years of working with thousands of managers and leaders, time and again the same barriers to delegating come up. These are very real reasons that need exploring so that delegating becomes your asset for success.

Everyone is already too busy!
I'm not sure they'll do it to my standard.
It's quicker if I just do it myself!

I don't want to cop the blame if it goes wrong, again!
I tried it once and I had to re-do all the work anyway.
I tried delegating but it all went pear-shaped.
I'm too busy to delegate!
I don't know what I can actually delegate to them.

Do any of these resonate with you? It's quite normal to identify with one or more of these barriers, especially if delegating is new to you or it didn't work for you in the past. In Table 1.3 are some tips to start shifting the barriers.

Table 1.3: Suggested tips to kick start removing barriers to delegating

WHAT MANAGERS SAY	QUICK TIP TO RESOLVE
Everyone is already too busy!	**Assumption:** Ask and be prepared to help them reprioritise.
I tried it once and I had to re-do all the work anyway.	**Process:** Milestones need to be agreed and set.
Everyone will think I'm being lazy or that I'll have nothing to do.	**Assumption:** Unless you're abdicating and dumping your own work on others, you will have enough work to do, now it'll be the right work.
I don't want to cop the blame if it goes wrong, again!	**Process:** Think and plan first! Stick to the plan! Agreed and set milestones ensures course correction when required. Issues are seen sooner rather than later.
It's quicker if I just do it myself!	**Correct:** in the short-term it is quicker but it will not be quicker in the long-term. **People:** Build stronger relationships and strengthen the trust. **Process:** Think and plan first!
I don't know what I can actually delegate to them.	Review your calendar and current workload for ideas. **Process:** Think and plan first!
I tried delegating but it all went pear-shaped.	**Process:** Think and plan! Stick to the plan!
I'm too busy to delegate!	**Assumption:** Stop! You do have 30 minutes to stop and review your workload. **Process:** Think and plan!
I'm not sure they'll do it to my standard.	**People:** Build stronger relationships and strengthen the trust. **Process:** Think and plan! Consider what your standards and expectations are before delegating.

In conversations with managers we explore these barriers further. Their fears about the process or outcomes of delegating become clear:

Who gets the blame if it doesn't work?
I just don't trust them.
It's too big a risk, I don't know how it will all turn out.
I don't want to be shown up: what if they're better than me?
Who gets the credit if it works?
I actually don't know how.
But I won't be in control.

Table 1.4, like Table 1.3, has suggested tips to help remove the fear-based barriers to delegating.

Table 1.4: Suggested tips to kick start removing fears of delegating

WHAT MANAGERS THINK AND FEEL	QUICK TIP TO RESOLVE
Who gets the blame if it doesn't work?	**Process:** Follow the plan to minimise risk.
I just don't trust them.	**People:** Build stronger relationships and strengthen trust. **Process:** Think and plan with a focus on matching the right person to task.
But I won't be in control!	**Assumption:** On the face of it it looks like you're handing over control however with the plan in place you hold control with the delegate.
Who gets the credit if it works?	Your success lies in their success! **Process:** Acknowledgement is essential to having people feel valued and therefore be prepared to step up again.
I don't want to be shown up: what if they're better than me?	Your success lies in their success! **Attitude:** It's about matching the right person for the task! It's a good thing that they are better at doing the task than anyone else: the right person for the right job! As a manager it's your job to help your team achieve. **People:** Build stronger relationships and strengthen the trust.
I actually don't know how.	Once you're finished reading this book you will know how! **Process:** Think, plan, implement!
It's too big a risk, I don't know how it will all turn out.	Nothing in life is 100% guaranteed but you can take methodical steps to minimise risk. **Process:** Think and plan! Stick to the plan!

It's critical to understand what you are thinking, feeling and fearing about delegating in order for you to take positive steps towards making delegation work for you. You need to know that acknowledging these is not a weakness; it's a sign of self-awareness, which is a significant component to quality self-leadership. Being able to identify and acknowledge your barriers to delegating gives you essential insights into, and information about what you can do to delegate more productively and confidently. This identification process saves you time and stress later when you start the nine steps to delegating.

If you want more proof that delegating is an essential function of your role, complete this equation:

1. Pick a task you already perform that you think you can delegate.

   [Has a boss already suggested you delegate something?]

   Example: Collate the end of month project hours.

TASK

2. How much time do you spend performing that task?

   Example: It takes 1.5 hours to chase up and collate project hours.

TIME

3. Convert that time to cost based on your hourly rate of pay.

   Example: 1.5 hours x $50 per hour = $75.

AMOUNT

4. Multiply that number by the number of times the task needs to be completed in a year to get an annual amount.

   Example: $75 x 12 months = $900.

AMOUNT

5. Calculate this cost based on a direct report completing the task.

   Example:
   Employee A is paid $35 per hour.
   1.5 hours x $35 = $52.50.
   $52.50 x 12 = $630.

AMOUNT

6. Calculate the saving.

   What's the difference between your cost and the direct report cost.

   Example: $900 - $630 = $270.

SAVING

BONUS:

You save the difference **plus** you have that time back to work on revenue generating tasks.

Example: $270 plus 18 hours (~ 2 work days) saved.

This is time that could be spent on longer term, revenue generating projects.

This is delegating one task, consider the cumulative effect when you delegate more tasks.

SELF-COACHING QUESTIONS

1. What stops you from delegating?

2. Thinking deeper about your responses above, what feelings are driving your reasons? What fears do you have?

3. If you have delegated before, what emotions did you experience through the process?

4. After reading through Tables 1.3 and 1.4 what insights do you now have that will help you feel more confident in delegating?

Spend the bulk of your time in your superpower - the things you love to do and excel at - and delegate the rest.

CHRISTINE KANE

FOUNDER & CEO UPLEVEL YOU

CHAPTER 6

TYPES OF DELEGATOR

Managers approach delegating based on their experiences, knowledge, expectations and viewpoints: from their past wins and bruises! If you can't work out where you are, why you are where you're at, it's so much harder to work out where to go, what to improve, and how to get there.

Maya Angelou's quote, "When you know better you do better." perfectly reflects delegation and leadership: know better, for example:

- yourself and your style of communication and leadership
- your experiences and reflections on delegating
- your relationships with your manager/boss and your team

... to know yourself better, and you will (at least you have the choice) to do better!

As you read through the types of delegators in Table 1.5 you may identify some elements in yourself and in other managers you know or have worked for/with.

Table 1.5: Types of Delegator and their Impact

Type of Delegator	Obstacle to Delegating	Focus Needed	Focus Activity	The Manager Feels	The Team Feels	Productivity
DISCERNING	NOT PLANNING	STRATEGY	HOW	SORTED OUT	ENGAGED	100%
DABBLING	NOT SEQUENCING	SYSTEM	WHEN	MISSING OUT	CONFUSED	60%
DICTATING	NOT TRUSTING	RELATIONSHIPS	WHO	WORN OUT	STIFLED	25%
DIRECTING	NOT BELIEVING	VALUE	WHY	BURNED OUT	BORED	10%
DISENGAGED	NOT KNOWING	LEARNING	WHAT	TUNED OUT	IGNORED	-10%

The Disengaged Delegator

This delegator has no clue: either they don't know how to delegate or aren't aware that they have the freedom to delegate.

Their obstacle to delegating is not knowing. Being made aware that they can delegate or what delegation is, is paramount to this manager boosting their productivity.

Chances are this delegator might feel tuned out and disconnected from their work, team, or the organisation. This could be driven by a lack of engagement or being way too busy. Either way productivity is impacted significantly. This delegator has their head down, buried in their work; when they walk around their head leads them because they are busy and constantly thinking of all the work that they need to get through, or hoping no one notices them.

The impact on the team can be that they can feel ignored. If the team is well established and the work is known, luck will be the key to the team getting on with their work. In most cases however, staff turnover will go up as boredom increases and the lack of opportunities, through delegating, will leave employees looking elsewhere.

The Directing Delegator

Like the conductor of an orchestra, the Director will give the orders. These delegators are busy, living on the edge of burn out, yet believe they are effective delegators because expected outcomes of the work are achieved, there's evidence of productivity.

This style of delegating can confuse, cause fear, or simply leave the team bored because they aren't engaged in the setting up of the delegation. Team members don't step up because they do not get the opportunity to build

a sense of ownership. E-v-e-r-y-t-h-i-n-g is directed from the manager. Over the long term, this can lead to some staff becoming increasingly reliant on the manager for problem-solving and basic thinking skills. This delegator may even think they are helping the team by doing all the thinking and planning for them. A good intention that actually doesn't get the results they expected. Work will get bottlenecked at the this delegators desk.

Without understanding the full process and the value delegating properly can produce within a team, this delegator will continue to feel burned out and the team unengaged.

The Dictating Delegator

This delegator gets work done but it comes at a high price for both the delegator and the team. Dictating work driven from a lack of trust means the team experiences significant amounts of micromanaging. They will most likely feel stifled and fear taking action: risk is not allowed.

This delegator hasn't taken the time to build solid, trusting, open and respectful relationships with their team and because this delegator doesn't really know whom they are working with, it makes sense that they feel they need a tighter level of control. More than task allocation this delegator also dictates when and how tasks will be performed and will be a constant presence checking everyone's progress, quality of work and even taking over if they feel they need to, which they will more often than not.

Similar to the Directing delegator the Dictator will often feel worn-out because they have to make sure everyone is doing their work. Micromanaging is exhausting for everyone. Tina Gilbertson[7] sums it up perfectly, "Someone who needs to control their environment, along with everyone in it, is someone who's motivated by fear. Even though they might give the opposite impression, micromanagers tend to be just plain scared most of the time."

The Dabbling Delegator

The Dabbling delegator uses an ad hoc approach. From one day to the next this delegator might pull a small team in to take over a project yet not delegate a full task or the right tasks that should be performed by more operational, skilled or appropriate staff.

This delegator lacks systematic organisation, which then leads to confusing their team. Big, complex projects may be delegated, but certain tasks within the project might be held back because this delegator doesn't have a clear picture of the successful outcome. When this delegator does delegate, the productivity of the whole team may go up, however this is very ad hoc. It might feel like a roller coaster ride for

[7] Tina Gilbertson, author of the forthcoming book Constructive Wallowing: How to Beat Bad Feelings by Letting Yourself Have Them

the team: some days you're up because opportunities to take on an exciting new task or project are delegated, and then other days are down because you can see an opportunity but this Dabbler doesn't delegate.

The Discerning Delegator

This delegator knows they can't do all the work required or expected. They carve out strategies and look for development opportunities through delegating to their team. This delegator understands the value of delegating as a means to engage their team. They know that with a delegation strategy and plan, engagement and productivity will increase.

This delegator actively seeks ways to engage the team early so the sense of ownership is strong and the team step up to the challenge of a new task or project.

SELF-COACHING QUESTIONS

1. Do you relate with anyone of the types of delegators, if so, which one?

....

....

....

....

2. Thinking about your favourite boss who has delegated to you previously, what type of delegator would you say they were? How did you feel during the delegation experience?

....

....

....

....

3. Thinking about your least favourite boss who has delegated to you previously, what type of delegator would you say they were? How did you feel during the delegation experience?

....

....

....

....

4. Reflecting deeper about your responses to questions two and three, what insights do you have about how you want to delegate going forward?

....

....

....

....

Being able to do everything in the business doesn't necessarily mean you should do everything.

K CALLAN

ACTRESS

CHAPTER 7

DELEGATION QUIZ

Read the following questions and place a tick in the box that best describes your answer:

	YES	NO
1. Do you find yourself spending more time than you would like on routine, administrative or menial tasks?		
2. Does your team rely on you for most decisions and problem solving?		
3. When you do delegate, do you spend time re-doing the work of others or worry about the level of care the employees take with the tasks?		
4. Do you spend significant time giving answers to questions that should already be known?		
5. Do you consistently have more work to do than time available?		
6. Do you worry about having time off (sick or recreation leave) as you're not sure the employees will run things properly while you're away?		
7. It feels impossible to delegate because everyone seems to be super busy already?		
8. You know that delegating would help improve productivity but you're not sure who will do the work to your standards?		
9. You feel an increase in stress levels when you do delegate and can't feel relaxed until the task is completed?		
10. Do you spend most of your day 'fire fighting' for your team rather than getting on with your work?		
Count up the number of ticks in the YES column		

If you have 8 - 10 YES ticks:

It's time to think about how you approach delegating and looking at the impact it's having on you and your team. Perhaps you may struggle with letting go or trusting your team, or prioritising your workload and time, and therefore you avoid delegating. Do you have past experiences where delegating hasn't worked, whether it was you delegating or someone delegated to you? Do you feel that the risk of success is too high? As you work through the rest of this book you will see how the nine steps will give you the structure and guidance, and as such, the confidence to be a discerning delegator.

If you have 4 - 7 YES ticks:

Well done, you're on your way to being an effective and productive delegator. You can see the potential delegating can have for achieving the results you need. Now you must learn the specific steps that will ensure you are making the most of opportunities to delegate and you are not getting in your own way of successful delegating.

If you have 0 - 3 YES ticks:

Great work! You are a productive delegator who knows that delegating is an effective function or strategy for developing your team and getting the work done. Consider ways you can use delegation as an opportunity to gather new ideas and approaches for carrying out work.

The really expert riders of horses let the horse know immediately who is in control, but then guide the horse with loose reins and seldom use the spurs.

SANDRA DAY O'CONNOR

FORMER ASSOCIATE JUSTICE OF THE SUPREME COURT, USA.

CHAPTER 8

BENEFITS OF DELEGATING

When managers micromanage and maintain strict control over their work and the work of their team they suffocate everyone and everything. The more practice managers have with delegating, the result is greater levels of confidence and a sense of freedom within their role and amongst the team. Figure one lays this out in a visual format for you:

Figure 1: Delegating and Its Benefits

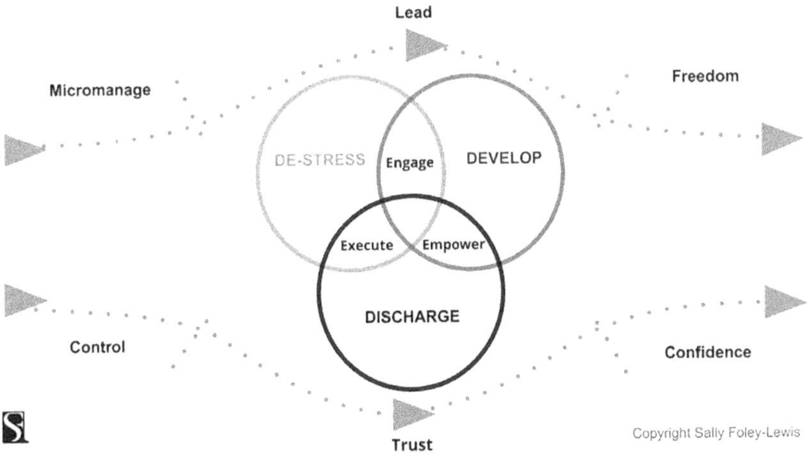

When you do delegate successfully, you have the opportunity to develop your people, and discharge tasks that you no longer should be doing. This de-stresses your environment because delegating well means that, collectively, you and the team are executing the work and through the delegation process you and the team are more engaged and empowered.

Managers who have a handle on delegating often report benefits such as:

- There's more time to do more important work
- There's more time to do more relevant work
- There's more time to think
- Work can carry on during a manager's absence: no bottlenecking of work and decisions
- Succession planning is supported because delegating prepares employees for higher duties
- The manager gains a reputation as a discerning, trusting delegator who develops their people

Employees also report how much more engaging and enjoyable work is when delegating has worked well:

- New skills can be developed
- New ideas can be explored
- Increased productivity through improved motivation and engagement
- Increased productivity through the allocation of tasks across a team
- Less frustration and delays (due to bottlenecking, i.e. waiting for decisions)
- Career progression

The flow-on effects of these benefits are felt at the organisational level too. Such as:

- Increased productivity
- Decreased human resourcing costs
- Employer of choice reputation
- Knowledge stays within the organisation longer as the right staff stay longer
- Succession planning is easier with greater potential for internal hiring

Whether you are an entrepreneur who hires only a few employees or you're a manager in a large organisation, delegation is an essential skill for success. According to a study conducted by Gallup[8], looking at CEOs with high delegator talent generated 33% greater revenue than those with lower levels of delegating skills.

With all these benefits, delegating is still one of the most under-utilised tools in a manager's skills toolkit. According to a study conducted by the Institute for Corporate Productivity[9], 46% of the 332 polled companies are concerned with their workers delegation skills, yet only 28% conduct delegation training.

If this resonates with you, and you can see your management team needs to build their delegation skills, buy them a copy of this book, or please reach out to organise a workshop: sally@sallyfoleylewis.com. *(Yep, a shameless plug!)*

---

[8] 2013 study conducted by Gallup. Results found in Delegating: A Huge Management Challenge for Entrepreneurs.

[9] Institute for Corporate Productivity (i4cp) in conjunction with HR.com conducted the Time Management Practitioner Consensus Survey in June 2007. Source: https://www.i4cp.com/news/2007/06/26/you-want-it-when

In a video highlighting the competitive advantage of delegating, Gail Thompson[10] reported that 53% of business owners believe they can grow their business by more than 20% if they delegate only 10% of their workload to someone else.

SELF-COACHING QUESTIONS

1. If you had a more developed team, how would this impact your workday today?

....

....

....

....

2. If you had a more engaged team, how would this impact your workday today?

....

....

....

....

[10] https://www.youtube.com/watch?v=2-m9OoOwZdM&feature=youtu.be linked in https://www.inc.com/peter-economy/delegate-for-competitive-advantage.html

3. With all other concerns taken care of, what would be your 10% workload that you would delegate?

4. What big goals, your big professional or work-based dreams or wishes, you'd love to bring to life if only you had more time?

Vulnerability is the birthplace of innovation, creativity and change.

BRENE BROWN

RESEARCH PROFESSOR AND AUTHOR OF MULTIPLE NEW YORK #1 BEST SELLING BOOKS

Don't delegate feedback you should be giving.
Don't delegate firing someone you should be firing.
Don't delegate another team's work to your team without prior consent.
STOP
Don't delegate high risk, sensitive or legal matters that require your leadership.
Don't delegate brand new initiatives that you need to perform or lead by example.
Don't delegate to someone who is on a performance management plan.

Don't delegate to someone who is already working to capacity.
Don't delegate management decisions you're expected to make.
Don't delegate to someone who is too new to the organisation or type of work to be done.
STOP
Don't delegate work that must be performed at your level of authority.
Don't delegate to someone who has expressly stated they do no want the opportunity or further development.
Don't delegate discipline that your role is expected to handle.

He who knows others is wise; he who knows himself is enlightened.

LAO TZU

PART
TWO

FOUNDATIONS OF DELEGATION SUCCESS

CHAPTER 9

SKILLS FOR DELEGATING

For any action, skills are needed to execute. Understanding what core skills are necessary for delegating helps you determine:

1. If you need to further develop any of these core skills,
2. How to engage your skills for delegating, and
3. The skills your direct reports need to develop further if delegating is or will be within the scope of their role.

Let's look at the essential skills you use to make delegating effective.

a. Interpersonal Communication

Being an effective communicator comes down to being able to create and send a message so that others understand in the manner intended. Listening for understanding, demonstrating presence and showing your interest is very much part of quality interpersonal communication skills.

Creating the message needs to be receiver focused, answering the question: how will it make sense for the delegate? Once you've constructed the message in a way that would best be understood, you need to select the right channel to deliver the message: face to face, email, video, work-sharing app or phone... with today's technology, you're not short on delivery options!

This is where planning your delegation can help you construct the right messages you want to send.

If distance or time zones impede the opportunity to meet face to face or over a video sharing platform, then a video or voice memo makes a really positive and effective option. The reason why video or voice is preferred is so that the delegate can see you and hear your tone of voice. You don't get this depth of communication from written formats, and written often leaves space for misinterpretation. Have you ever read an email reply and thought, *"That is totally* ***not*** *what I meant!"*?

By seeing you or hearing the tone of your voice, they can gauge your personality and intent, which is advantageous for understanding the importance of, and your enthusiasm for the task or project. Creating a voice memo gives scope and space for deeper explanation because as the speaker, it's through speaking you can hear yourself better than if you were writing, and can adjust to ensure increased logic and flow in your message. Have you ever read your writing out aloud and realised it wasn't as clear or logical as you first thought?

If it takes approximately 90 seconds to establish a rapport when you make a first encounter with someone[11], then your tone - be it in voice or written - will make a big difference to how the delegate receives the delegation. You have no doubt heard the saying: *"It's not what you say, it's how you say it!"* This matters!

---

[11] Nicholas Boothman, keynote speaker, and author of How to Make People likeLike You in 90 Seconds or Less

Making the communication as personable as possible will also increase the chances of a successful delegation, and will break down barriers to communication should issues arise.

Listening gives you clues as to what you can do to improve processes, systems and relationships.

When you listen carefully, you demonstrate respect, care and concern for the other person. This encourages that person to feel comfortable enough to contribute further to the conversation.

Listening and observing means you can more easily detect someone feeling resistant to taking on a delegation. Showing you are prepared to, and actually are a good listener, opens the door for the delegate to feel safe to raise issues earlier rather than later.

A wonderful resource for helping you learn to listen deeply is the book, *Deep Listening: Impact Beyond Words* by Oscar Trimboli.

b. Emotional Intelligence

Emotional intelligence is about self- and social-awareness, empathy, motivation, control or regulation and the expression of emotions (social skills). Essentially it's about knowing how to behave and respond towards others. In the context of delegating, your emotional intelligence keeps your emotions in check while you are re-allocating or letting go of tasks, during the delegation as it progresses, and if something goes wrong.

Delegating tasks or projects, especially those tasks you have been doing for some time and enjoy doing, can be hard to let go of. These may be tasks you took with you when you were promoted into a managerial role or they simply remained with you during organisational change. You have owned them and enjoyed them; so obviously, it's a challenge to part ways with them now. Knowing that freeing yourself up to do work far more aligned with your role, or to your future role, means letting go.

Your ability to keep your emotions in check ensures you can communicate from a position of objectivity and empathy.

Many great books have been written about emotional intelligence. I recommend that if you want to continually improve your understanding of, and control over your emotional intelligence, start with the classic book, *Emotional Intelligence: Why It Can Matter More Than IQ* by Daniel Goleman. Two other books that complement the improvement of emotional intelligence are *Mindset: How You Can Fulfill Your Potential* by Dr Carol S. Dweck and *Grit: The Power of Passion and Perseverance* by Angela Duckworth.

Being able to regulate your emotions is not the same as not feeling frustrated, angry, disappointed, delighted or happy. It's about being aware of these emotions, and understanding what they mean and not letting them drive the communication. Additionally, emotional intelligence includes identifying how the delegate may feel and having empathy for them throughout the delegation process. Great delegators can notice the delegate's emotions and acknowledge or validate them. Everyone, yes, you too, are entitled to their emotions and are not immune from them; it's how they are handled that determines a successful outcome.

c. Asking Quality Questions

Asking quality questions goes hand in hand with listening in order to gather quality information. Ask questions that encourage conversations and the whole delegation to flow.

Examples of questions that encourage a delegation set-up conversation to flow:

- What impact do you think this task or project will have on our business?
- What impact do you think this task or project will have on our team?
- What impact do you think this task or project will have on your day today?
- What are your thoughts on what success in this project will look like?
- How long do you think this will take to complete?
- What resources do you think you'll need to complete the task or project?
- What would your action plan for this task or project look like?
- What milestones do we need so we are confident of progress?
- What will get in your way of success?
- Who needs to know you're taking on this task or project?
- Who can help you?
- How can I support you best?
- How do you feel about this task or project?
- What other priorities do you have right now that might be impacted upon by this task or project, or would influence this task or project?
- Is there anyone else in the team who is ready to learn what you do and could take on part of your existing work as a development opportunity?
- Is there anyone else in the team whom you know is keen to develop skills in this area?
- What do you need me to do to keep you accountable or on track through the delegation?

Examples of questions to ask during the delegation process:

- What's working well for you?
- What's not going as well as you'd planned?
- What are you learning so far in this process?
- Given the progress to date, how can I best continue to support you?
- What will keep you motivated to keep going?
- What surprises have emerged along the way so far, and what have you learned?
- Have you had to course-correct, how has that worked out for you?
- Have any other ideas or opportunities emerged from this task or project?
- What have you tried so far?
- Have you got all the resources you need?
- What would make sense to do next?
- How is our organisational culture affecting your progress?

Examples of questions to ask after the delegation process:

- What went well?
- What lessons have you learned from doing this task or project?
- What skills have you developed?
- What are you most proud of?
- If we were to delegate this task to someone else, how would we do it better?
- If we were to delegate this task to someone else, whom do you think is ready for the opportunity?
- What ideas or opportunities emerged from doing this work?

- What could we/you do next?
- What didn't work? What did we/you learn about this not working?
- What resources did you need more or less of during the delegation?
- What impact does our organisational culture have on this delegation?

d. Flexibility

Being flexible is about understanding and being able to adapt should the task or project, once started, turns out to be the wrong work to do or fails before it really takes off. Sometimes you need to start the work to then understand what will or won't work or what information is missing. Be ready for that to possibly happen.

Flexibility allows you to course-correct, delay or delete so that there are minimal negative impacts to the work, team, delegate, you and the organisation. Being flexible means you also have the emotional intelligence to not let frustration get the better of you if the task fails, the delegate leaves or doesn't perform.

Give yourself and the delegate time to have quality and effective conversations without feeling rushed. This means you will achieve productive and positive outcomes sooner rather than later. Flexibility now saves you time, money and your sanity later.

e. Problem Solving

In the set up and throughout the delegation, it's important to find ways to help the delegate do their own problem solving. Avoid giving answers immediately. Even if you know the right answer, stop! Let the delegate think. Don't cave in to the pressure to speed through the delegation conversation.

Having excellent problem-solving skills means, firstly, being able to identify clearly what the real problem (task/project) is, and then breaking it down into manageable chunks of single or smaller tasks. While you knowing this is excellent, it gives you the confidence that you can guide rather than dictate or direct the delegate.

Task allocation can be relatively straightforward however there will be times when there is a problem to solve. You may know the desired outcome and can identify a development opportunity for one of your direct reports. Be mindful to look for the opportunity for the delegate to strengthen their own problem solving skills. Present the project or task as a problem, at least initially, rather than the desired solution to the desired outcome.

An example would be:

1. **Solution disguised as a problem:** *We need more space in this office.*

2. **Problem identification:** *The workspace is cluttered and congested.*

1. **Solution disguised as a problem:** *We need better run meetings.*

2. **Problem identification:** *Our meetings don't seem to be effective anymore. Our meetings run overtime.*

Giving a solution, when there's an opportunity for more creative and innovative thinking from the delegate, hinders deeper engagement in how the task or project can be achieved or completed successfully. When the task or project can be presented as a problem, you can spend time generating ideas with the delegate and you might be surprised with what extra ideas emerge.

Emotional intelligence, asking quality questions, listening, flexibility and problem solving are the foundational skills for successful delegation. Fine-tuning these skills will benefit you in more ways than just delegating - they are skills for leadership and life.

SELF-COACHING QUESTIONS

1. Score your skill level out of 10: 1 being no skill and 10 being skill master:

Interpersonal Communication Skills	_ / 10
Emotional Intelligence Skills	_ / 10
Asking Quality Questions Skills	_ / 10
Flexibility	_ / 10
Problem Solving Skills	_ / 10

2. What are your top three skills?

....

....

....

3. Reflecting deeper about your top three skills, how did you get to be so good with these skills that could help you further develop your lowest three skills?

....

....

....

....

4. What will you do to further develop your lowest three scoring skills?

Control leads to compliance; autonomy leads to engagement.

DANIEL H. PINK

AUTHOR OF “DRIVE” AND “WHEN”

CHAPTER 10

TRUST AND RELATIONSHIPS

The performance of individuals, teams and organisations rely on trust. Trust, as a basic definition for the purposes of delegating, is a willingness to accept risk based on someone else's behaviour[12]. No two people are going to have the same level of tolerance for risk so it's essential to build trust through the determinants of trustworthiness: competency, integrity, empathy and rapport. Trust and trustworthiness are connected: when someone decides to trust another they will do so based on that person's trustworthiness.

For ensuring delegating is successful, start with building a rapport, a quality working relationship with those you wish to involve in delegating. The time spent getting to know the team is not wasting time socialising when it's time invested in understanding how the team members like to work, communicate, learn and achieve.

---

[12] Borum, Randy, "The Science of Interpersonal Trust" (2010). Mental Health Law & Policy Faculty Publications. 574. http://scholarcommons.usf.edu/mhlp_facpub/574

Look at the skills, attitudes and capacities of the team: identifying who is capable and who has the potential based on skills needed to complete a task or project. If you accurately match skills to a task you can create an environment you can trust going forward. If you can identify team members who might not have the skills, yet the potential, your support and guidance to help them build the skills, will also help positively grow trust.

Who is reliable, responsible and demonstrates a level of care or empathy for their work, the team and the organisation? People who demonstrate these characteristics are most likely going to trigger greater levels of trust, which then makes the willingness (risk) to delegate easier. Employees who seem to lack these trust building characteristics need to be handled differently before delegating is to be successful: focus on performance, reliability and responsibility first. You might delegate a small task to build reliability, responsibility and attention to detail.

Successful delegating relies on trust in both directions: you need to trust the delegate and the delegate needs to trust you. As a delegator are you competent at delegating (you're reading this book so that's a yes! Or you're well on your way!); are you reliable and responsible; do you walk your talk; do you care, show empathy for the team, the work, the organisation; do you take time to build relationships? Essentially, can the team and the delegate, trust you?

If you struggle to trust a delegate, you are more likely to be pulled into micromanaging, which can have a costly effect on the work and relationships.

SELF-COACHING QUESTIONS

1. Who do you need to build a stronger relationship or build a rapport with?

2. What will you do to further demonstrate your integrity and empathy as the manager of your team?

3. What are three things about you that your team doesn't know that you're happy for them to know, and would contribute to strengthening the relationship with the team members?

Trust is earned when actions meet words.

CHRIS BUTLER

MUSICIAN AND WRITER

CHAPTER 11

A WORD ON MICROMANAGING

Don't!

That's the word on micromanaging!

Micromanaging happens because performance has not been up to standard; there's a fear that details or deadlines will be missed; or something has happened where the manager perceives a need to step in and do what's in their power to get the work done. The micromanager acts in order to minimise perceived or possible loss or negative consequences. Determining standards, details or perceiving when something might go wrong is subjective. Fear, and fear of the unknown, underpins this.

In delegating, micromanaging will occur if you skip the essential steps and don't have a quality trusting relationship. Where steps are skipped too many assumptions will be made regarding the desired outcome, skills and capacity to take on the task or project. Task or project timing will be messed up as micromanaging creates excessive work, meetings and frustrations. Assuming, skipping or being vague about any or all of these steps will lead to issues that require management stepping in to micromanage. Working through a plan minimises the fear of the unknown.

Alternatively, micromanaging occurs because the manager simply is not aware of any other way to manage and lead the team. Following the delegation nine steps (described in detail in part three), diligently will provide the delegator with the structure to build skills, knowledge, trust and confidence in their delegating and in their delegates.

Deciding what not to do is as important as deciding what to do.

JESSICA JACKLY

CO-FOUNDER OF KIVA

CHAPTER 12

SLOW IS FAST

From an old Latin line, *festina lente*, or *hurry slowly*, is the notion that if you do things too fast you're likely to waste time going back to correct mistakes. To hurry slowly is to work carefully and methodically and it'll be the fastest way to achieve the desired outcome.

If delegating successfully has eluded you in the past or you've avoided delegating for any manner of reason, follow the nine steps in Part Three. Give yourself permission to work through each step carefully and methodically so you can guarantee a successful outcome.

Download and use the templates to guide you and once you are confident you have the steps in hand, you will, like learning anything, find the process flows ever more quickly and smoothly.

"I don't have time" is a common phrase managers say based on their normal, hectic day to day, let alone being able to delegate. Understanding how long you take to complete tasks is critical for your productivity, results and happiness.

If you truly struggle with having time to delegate, these will help you:

- Complete a time log: for two weeks track where you spend your time. Time logs are incredible for highlighting what consumes your time. Be honest with yourself, the more accurate you are with your time log the more value it will be for you. Besides, no one else needs to see it! Once you can see how you spend your time it often reveals where you can reduce wastage.
- Schedule time to think into your day, everyday! It only needs to be a small amount of time yet it gives you incredible peace and space to think and plan your day or week or delegations. Many managers I work with schedule anywhere from 10 minutes to 45 minute of 100% thinking and planning time per day. It all comes down to whether your day rules you or you rule your day.
- Read *The Productive Leader: How to Achieve More, Reduce Stress and Gain 2 Hours Per Day*: https://www.sallyfoleylewis.com/books/the-productive-leader/ … Sure, a shameless plug for my book but it does provide insight, tips and strategies for improving personal productivity as well as helping your team be more productive.

When you hurry slowly, which is really me tell you to stop and plan, you will gain so many more benefits to your delegating:

1. The delegating process will stay on course giving you and the delegate a greater sense of control.
2. The objective - the desired outcome - will be clear or you'll have the right environment to ensure clarity.
3. While planning will include some 'educated guessing', it'll be more accurate the more you do it.

4. Delegating priorities, that is, who does what and when, will be more obvious.
5. Work will be completed on time more often, and cost far less.
6. Tracking performance will become much easier, you'll chase up less because you both agree on tracking.
7. You'll start to see budget improvements.
8. Course correction will be easier, faster and cheaper as issues and hiccups will be seen sooner and not be left, hidden, or be harder and costlier to fix.

Slow is fast! You owe it to yourself and your team.

The first rule of management is delegation. Don't try and do everything yourself because you can't.

ANTHEA TURNER

UK TELEVISION PRESENTER

CHAPTER 13

RESPONSIBILITY AND AUTHORITY

Clarity regarding responsibility and authority is essential for a successful outcome. Who has the ultimate responsibility for a task or project? And, at what point does your authority shift to the employee (or delegate)? You need to answer these two questions in order to minimise micromanaging, avoid bottlenecking, delays to progress, and to empower both the manager and employee.

What is responsibility in the context of delegating?

Responsibility is duty, obligation and being accountable for work being done for a determined outcome.

Who has responsibility?

As the team leader, department manager, the person in charge, you will have the ***overall*** responsibility with a shared task responsibility. It's the employee's responsibility to get the job done and it's also your responsibility to ensure the work gets done. The 'buck does stop with you', which makes sense that trust is essential. You cannot delegate all the responsibility away.

What is authority in the context of delegating?

Power and **rights** to act, to decide, to implement, to execute, describes authority in the context of delegating.

Who has authority?

As the delegator, you give or hand over authority to the delegate in order to complete the task or project. If you delegate everything except authority then you risk micromanaging, creating delays, stalling progress and sending the message that you don't trust your employee.

Where your authority ends and the delegate's authority takes over can be challenging to work out at times, however you can discuss this and negotiate how much authority each of you have as a project unfolds.

Talking about responsibility and authority need to be part of the delegation conversation. Being explicit about the level and degree of responsibility and authority reduces the risk of erroneous assumptions and provides a strong foundation for the work to be done accurately and timely.

In cases where new projects or tasks are being delegated, it can be somewhat stressful knowing how much responsibility and authority to hand over: it's the fear of the unknown. You will no doubt have some level of concern for how this will work out, and what you and the delegate need to do. With strong, open and respectful relationships in place, it's much easier to discuss the concerns of the unknown and to work together to break the project down into smaller tasks that can be executed.

If you are struggling with handing over responsibility and authority, then go back and focus on the relationship you have with the delegate and consider further trust building.

In the 1950s, in the profession of project management, the term **RACI** Matrix (*Ray-see*). was introduced. RACI stands for Responsible, Accountable, Consulted and Informed. In project management, RACI breaks down the actions and assigns the relevant people. Here is a simple example:

Team End of Year Celebration

	PERSON A	PERSON B	PERSON C	PERSON D
Select Date	R/A	C	C	C
Select Time	R/A	C	C	C
Select Venue	R	A	I	I
Book Venue	R	A		
Promote Event	I	R/A	I	I

R - Responsible A - Accountable C - Consulted I - Informed

While the RACI matrix provides detail and gives certainty as to who is responsible and accountable it helps to ensure that you consult the right stakeholders. Therefore, it is a solid check and balance when working through your delegation plan; especially at step three (see Part Three of this book). At the very least, you can use the acronym RACI to ensure you have considered who needs to be ultimately responsible (this will most likely be you most of the time), responsible for the task or project, accountable, consulted and informed.

SELF-COACHING QUESTIONS

1. Think about the last time you were given responsibility for something, how did you feel? What more information would you have wanted before taking on the responsibility?

2. Have you ever had a boss who didn't trust you? Did they give you the right level of responsibility for the work? Did you have the right level of authority to get on with the work? If they did or did not, how did you feel?

3. Reflecting deeper about your responses to questions one and two, what insights do you now have from the experiences that will help your delegate successfully?

An hour of planning can save you 10 hours of doing.

DALE CARNEGIE

AUTHOR: HOW TO WIN FRIENDS AND INFLUENCE PEOPLE

PART THREE

HOW TO DELEGATE

NINE STEPS TO DELEGATING

To make delegating successful, it makes sense to break it down into smaller steps. Nine steps may seem like a lot but once you work through each one you'll see how common sense they are, and with practice may only take a few minutes to check each step in your delegating. Dividing the nine steps, it covers three phases: before, during and after; and into three categories: Task (what), People (whom) and Process (how). See Figure 2.

Figure 2: Nine Steps to Delegating Success

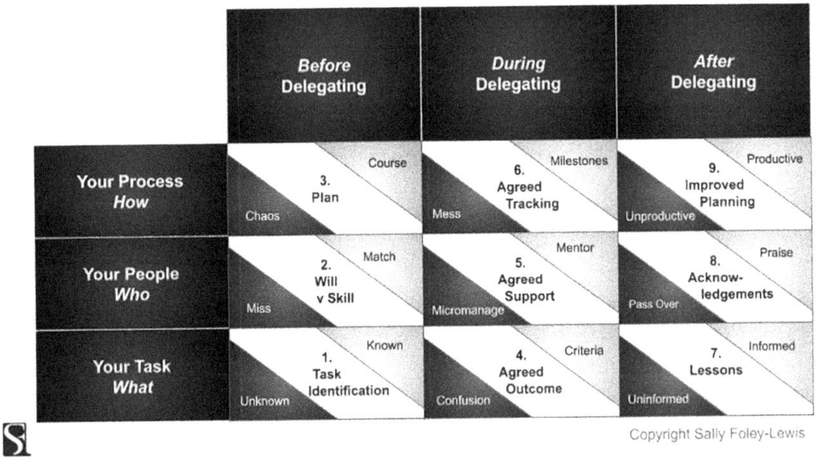

Before Delegating
During Delegating
After Delegating
Your Process How
Chaos
3. Plan
Course
Mess
6. Agreed Tracking
Milestones
Unproductive
9. Improved Planning
Productive
Your People Who
Miss
2. Will v Skill
Match
Micromanage
5. Agreed Support
Mentor
Pass Over
8. Acknow-ledgements
Praise
Your Task What
Unknown
1. Task Identification
Known
Confusion
4. Agreed Outcome
Criteria
Uninformed
7. Lessons
Informed
Copyright Sally Foley-Lewis

You can download the Nine Steps to Delegating Success model at **https://www.sallyfoleylewis.com/delegate-book-downloads/**

Broken down into steps ensures that there is every chance of success. It also means that for a first-time delegator or first time following this suggested process, it will take time. New or experienced, remember that *hurry slowly* still applies! With practice, the process will speed up. Missing steps leads to much greater chances of mistakes occurring, costly delays and unnecessary re-work.

Let's go...

BEFORE DELEGATING

To plan your delegation means you will avoid dumping the wrong task on the wrong person while you're rushing from one meeting to the next. Planning can cause some people's eyes to glaze over, while at the other extreme others love it so much that they spend their entire time planning and neglect to implement their plans. Whether you fall into one of these two types of 'planners,' or somewhere in between, planning is essential for your success. The success of delegating is your planning. In the Before Delegating phase there are three key steps:

1. Your Task: What - Task Identification

What is the task you will delegate? Sometimes you might identify that someone has some capacity in his or her workload or desire to take on more work, which might help determine the task you will delegate to that person.

Known or Unknown

If you know what the task is, but it's new to you and the team, i.e. you've not done this exact type of task before, this presents you with the amazing opportunity to collaborate with your team: giving the group a chance to shine! Smaller actions that lead to task completion will be the better way to delegate so that milestones can be set and progress checked until there is greater confidence from the experience. A new project can be exciting but it can also trigger concerns based on the fear of the unknown: How do we do this? How will this turn out? Rather than delegate the whole task or project away, collaborate instead!

Writing down notes describing the task will help give you confidence that you are clear on what is to be done.

If you are not sure if you can delegate a task, use the task decision flowchart to determine if you can or not:

Figure 3: Task Decision Flowchart

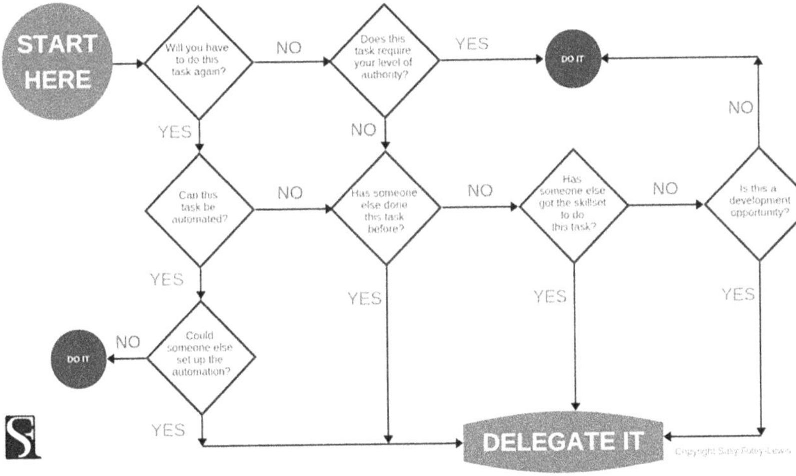

You can download the Task Decision Flowchart at
https://www.sallyfoleylewis.com/delegate-book-downloads/

2. Your People: Who - Will Versus Skill

Who is the best person to undertake the delegated task? To answer this you might consider the following qualifying questions:

Capability to perform the delegated task:

- Who has experience of doing this exact task before? *[Direct experience]*
- Who has the experience of doing work like this task before? *[Has the skills]*

Capacity to perform the delegated task:

- Who has time to take on this delegated task? *[Don't assume]*
- Who has asked for more work and has the time to take on more? *[Be sure this person performs their standard work and is not asking for more as a diversion, simply to please, or they are unable to hold healthy boundaries.]*

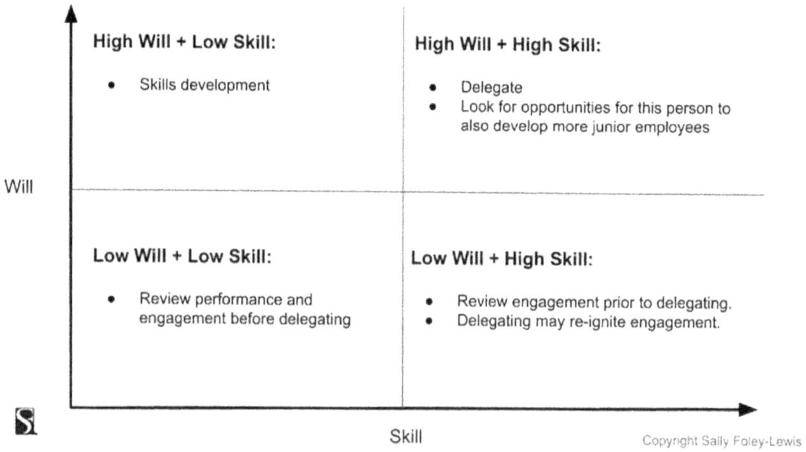
High Will + Low Skill:
Skills development
High Will + High Skill:
Delegate
Look for opportunities for this person to also develop more junior employees
Will
Low Will + Low Skill:
Review performance and engagement before delegating
Low Will + High Skill:
Review engagement prior to delegating.
Delegating may re-ignite engagement.
Skill
Copyright Sally Foley-Lewis

Matching the right person to the right task could be simple, obvious and straightforward: you know that the best person to tame a lion is a lion tamer. Yet there will be times where matching task and person might not be quite so straightforward. This is why strong, trusting relationships with your direct reports make matching easier.

Listening to and observing your people gives you additional information about what they can, could or can't handle.

Low Will + Low Skill:

If you have someone who has a low level of skill and lacking the will to do more, then you most likely need to do some deeper investigation. For starters, check that you have the right person in the right role, without adding any further work or opportunities to this employee's workload. I advise that you consider reallocating this person to a more appropriate role or reallocating tasks in order to help skill this person up to standard. It's in these challenging situations where a thorough recruiting process shows its value.

High Will + Low Skill:

When someone has a high level of enthusiasm to do more yet a low level of relevant skills, this presents a potential development opportunity. You can step in and show the person how to execute the task. Alternatively, you can empower a high potential - someone you identified as ready for more responsibility and more leadership potential - who also has the skills to show the person. This is where delegating becomes a very cost effective learning and development opportunity.

Low Will + High Skill:

An employee, whom you determine has all the skills available for delegation, yet lacks the will or enthusiasm, might already be working at full capacity and unable to take on more work. The Low Will + High Skill employee may not be aware that they can ask for more opportunities or you've assumed that they are not keen or have the capacity. Check what assumptions might be at play in this scenario: you may find that discussing an opportunity to take on a special project might reignite motivation.

Alternatively, you may have someone who's only suited to their current role:

> *Sascha has been in the same position for more than 25 years. She loves her job and is exceptional at it. She's seen many bosses come and go over her 25 years. The one mainstay is what Sascha does: she has been clear throughout her career that she loves what she does but does not want more, nor less either. Essentially, she doesn't want to climb any career ladder or take on extra responsibilities.*
>
> *Without taking the time to know Sascha, and see her perform it could be easy to assume she's unwilling and has limited skills. This is simply not true. When it comes to delegation, you simply skip Sascha. It would be wise though to check in with Sasha from time to time in case she does want to take on something new. The better Sascha's boss knows Sascha the boss is best placed to ensure Sascha is only approached for tasks and projects that she would really be keen to take on.*

High Will + High Skill:

Ultimately, the easiest person to delegate to is the one with all the right skills - even the same experiences - and has the enthusiasm and the capacity in their day to tackle more. This employee may even be best placed to participate in skilling the High Will + Low Skill employee if the opportunity and timing are available. This gives you the context to see how ready your High Will + High Skill is for higher duties or promotion. This also presents an opportunity for you to demonstrate your trust in them.

Discharge or Develop

In determining the right person to take on the delegation, it might be obvious that one person would be a logical candidate; you simply need to discharge the task. However, you might have an opportunity for development in the delegation, and you can handle this in one of two ways:

Option 1:

You delegate the task to someone who has the skills but not the exact experience, and encourage them to undertake the task or project as a development opportunity. If they are not sure (potentially presenting as unwilling), be sure to highlight the value this opportunity presents for them: *what's in it for them.*

You will also need to help the delegate see they have the skills on board, even though they haven't the experience.

Option 2:

You discharge the task to someone who's willing and skilled, Delegate A, and identify another employee, Delegate B, who would value the learning or development opportunity from the task or project. Delegate A now has a leadership development opportunity. As the manager, you will need to support Delegate A in their leadership first, and the task or project second. This option would work well when you have employees who have a High Will + High Skill and there are limited promotional opportunities. If you have an employee who is highly skilled but seems unwilling, if the drive of that unwillingness is from boredom, this option of empowering them to develop other team members could re-engage the employee and improve productivity.

Fundamentally, be sure you are taking every opportunity not to simply discharge tasks, but also use delegation for development; and you can invite greater involvement through highlighting the value to the employees/delegates.

What's In It For Them?

Even if you have a very enthusiastic and skilled employee ready to take on a task or project, it's advisable to consider what's in it for them to do the work. Will it be a means to further develop a skill; or a way to help the team get through an unusually busy period; or help a new employee pick up some skills quickly?

Have you ever had someone tell you that they admire a certain skill or characteristic about you yet it wasn't obvious to you? If an employee is not sure about taking on a delegation, having pre-considered the benefits for them will make the delegation conversation far more effective. It can be a way to demonstrate your faith and trust in them, even if they can't see it in themselves.

3. Your Process: How - The Plan

With the task and the person identified, you have started to set the course for success. Without planning, you would be running a big risk of having chaos. Without planning, the execution of the delegation is left to assumptions that may lead to the wrong outcomes or procrastination, which leads to nothing or the wrong work being achieved.

Being clear about what success looks like for you, the delegate and the actual work starts with having a plan. Delegation in itself is a project. According to research conducted by the Project Management Institute[13] (PMI), only 26% of projects succeed. PMI stated that running too many projects at once, inconsistency and rework factored into project failure. Without thorough planning:

---

[13] https://www.pmi.org/-/media/pmi/documents/public/pdf/learning/thought-leadership/pulse/pulse-of-the-profession-2017.pdf

- It's impossible to determine the real level of capacity to take on a delegation;
- The output through the delegation could quickly become inconsistent, especially if people are left waiting or are procrastinating; and
- Rework would undoubtedly have to happen in order to ensure an eventual, and yet more costly, successful outcome.

The delegation plan needs to include more than the task and the person. A successful plan endeavours to address all areas and cover all foreseeable contingencies. The plan includes:

- Task or project description
- This is why this task or project is important
- What success looks like
- Deadline and milestones
- Resources available (and not available)
- Stakeholders: who will be affected by the outcome; who can be of help to execute; this also helps to prevent bottlenecking should a stakeholder come to you rather than the delegate for an answer related to the task or project (RACI)
- What roadblocks could possibly hinder success

Your Delegation Plan is starting to look like this:

TASK IDENTIFICATION:

Give a thorough description of the task or project. It is better to have more information than not enough.

PURPOSE:

Why does this task or project needs to be executed? What is its importance? Answering these helps the delegate to understand the value of the delegation and task or project, and to take more ownership. This leads to more engagement and investment in a successful outcome.

WILL VERSUS SKILL:

Who is the best person to undertake this task or project? Is this simply task allocation or a development opportunity? What skills are needed and what skills might need to be developed? Is there capacity to undertake this task or project or will other work need to be re-prioritised?

- Task Allocation
- Development Opportunity (You will develop via delegation)
- Delegate Could Develop Someone else

WHAT'S IN IT FOR THEM:

Why should the delegate take on this task or project? What will the delegate gain from doing this work?

STAKEHOLDERS:

Who will be affected by the outcome of the task or project?

Who will be affected while this task or project is being executed?

Who needs to know the delegate is responsible for this task or project?

So that the right people know who to go to during the course of the delegation: Who needs to know?

HAVE YOU IDENTIFIED WHO IS...

Responsible

Accountable

Consulted

Informed

RESOURCES AVAILABLE:

What resources are at the delegate's disposal to execute the task or project? These can include other people, physical resources, budget, external source, etc. It is essential to never assume the delegate will know what they can or cannot use or spend.

Caylon was asked to take on an exciting new project as a trial. If the project were a success, it would be rolled out nationally. Sara and Caylon discussed the project briefly and going by Caylon's enthusiasm, Sara assumed the project would be in safe hands and she felt confident that Caylon was the right person for the task! Both Sara and Caylon neglected to discuss what resources Caylon could tap into to run the project, and without setting milestones along the way, the project was months down the track with a $50,000 bill - ouch! Sara assumed that Caylon knew he had to ask for approval for expenses over $1,000. So when Caylon wasn't asking, Sara, assumed he was going well by keeping costs right down. An expensive lesson, made even more painful because the project itself was excellent but much tougher to sell to senior leadership because milestones were not set in order to pick up issues early, and resources were not clarified.

You can find your complete Delegation Plan Template at **https://www.sallyfoleylewis.com/delegate-book-downloads/**

DURING DELEGATING

Once the delegation has started, you simply cannot disappear! Being accessible during the delegation means you can step in quickly if a problem arises that needs your level of authority or expertise. Furthermore, your presence can provide a sense of support for the delegate. During the delegation, there are three key elements to ensure you stay engaged in the process: outcome, support and tracking.

4. Your Task: What - Agreed Outcomes

Have you ever been in a conversation with someone and after a few minutes, you suddenly realise you are both talking about two completely different things? It might be funny when the topic is not too critical or when in a social context but when it's at work, about work, where confusion leads to potentially big costs - money, safety, job security - it's a little less funny!

This is why planning pays off for you. Because you have taken some time to plan and think about what success looks like for the delegation, you are in a much better place to describe the task or project so that the delegate is also clear. Together you and the delegate can set criteria, standards, expectations and agreements. Together you can confirm you are both on the same page when it comes to what success looks like. To do this successfully, it's imperative to ask the delegate clarifying questions. Simply asking: "Do you understand the task?" can create problems:

a. It can sound derogatory asking the question in that way, despite any pleasant and supportive tone you may use.

b. If there are culture or language differences, asking the question this way limits the potential to actually hear back what's expected in order to confirm understanding: it's a closed question and it may lead to a simple, "yes." This "yes" might be a cover up to avoid being perceived as incompetent or said because of a perception that "yes" is the right answer to give.

Whilst living abroad, a friend of mine had a maid/housekeeper who spoke (broken) English as their third language. When my friend wanted to give her maid a specific cleaning task, she described the task and then asked, "Do you understand?". The helper simply replied, "Yes, Madam." The reality is that the helper really did not understand, as the specific task was not completed. Unfortunately, this happened regularly until my friend realised she needed to ask the same question in a more effective way.

Alternative ways to essentially ask the same question yet more thoroughly check understanding could be:

"So that I'm sure I've told you everything, and not forgotten anything, can you tell me in your words what the outcome of this task/project should be?"

"When it comes to achieving the outcome, what information have I missed out?"

"What does a successful outcome of this task/project look like to you?"

In your Delegation Plan Template it will look like this:

A SUCCESSFUL OUTCOME LOOKS LIKE…

Describe what a successful outcome will look like. Having this clear helps to ensure both you and the delegate are working from the same understanding.

You can find your complete Delegation Plan Template at
https://www.sallyfoleylewis.com/delegate-book-downloads/

5. Your Task: Who - Agreed Support

This step of delegating can be the toughest for some managers; this is why trust and strong quality relationships are so essential for delegating to be successful.

Aristotle is quoted as saying, "All that we do is done with an eye to something else." Thinking about this in the context of supporting a delegate trying to get on with the task or project should highlight that a lack of trust leads to a sense of needing more control that then drives a manager to micromanage.

Without trust, it's easy to be pulled into a micromanaging style: it even makes sense that if a manager doesn't trust the delegate, of course they will be hovering and interfering every single step of the way. This serves no one and might even lead to rework, task or project failure, diminished performance, turnover or reverse delegation (which is covered later in this book).

Agreeing support should be based on how the delegate wants to be supported. Let the delegate give you direction, at least to start the agreement process.

> *Sharon, the Head of the Department, had a task she wanted to delegate to Chris. She had worked through the delegation plan and when it came to agreeing the level of support, Sharon told Chris that she wanted to meet daily to check progress and to provide support. Chris felt as though the level of support was not open for negotiation based on the way Sharon had communicated so he left the delegation meeting feeling Sharon didn't trust him.*
>
> *"She didn't really ask me my thoughts on the task, I'm happy she's handing it over to me because I feel as though I'm the right person to take it on, but to meet daily to support me is over the top. Had she asked me, I would have suggested another meeting right after I've done the first part of the task once and then agreed to the next level of support required. I know she wants it to go well, so do I, but this is just micromanaging!"*

Taking on the role of a coach or mentor to provide support during the delegation allows you to provide advice when required; demonstrate or train when needed; challenge assumptions that might be limiting progress; and inspire for continued performance.

To agree on how to support someone throughout the delegation, consider asking the delegate what support they want. Start with asking so that you can gauge the level of confidence the delegate has regarding the task or project and you can shift to more or less based on the starting point the delegate has suggested.

But… I hear you say…

What if they don't want any support?

If the delegate is willing and highly skilled then they may not actually need a lot, if any, extra support from you. If you want to give them support, you might want to reflect on what's driving that need for you: what's your motivation behind wanting or needing to give support? Is that about trust, control or some other concern? Once you can identify the concern, that is the issue you will need to address, for and in yourself, first.

If you are confident that the delegate needs your support more than they state they need, offer to start with a higher level of support and review that support as the task or project continues. You will need to own your desire for offering support, you might want to share your concerns and you will reach a better outcome if you also show you're prepared to step back as the tracking shows positive results. This is where your flexibility comes into play.

What if they want too much support?

If a delegate suggests a level of support that you consider more than what would be required or necessary, take the time to address that with them. Investigate why they feel they need so much support: is it a lack of confidence, limited experience, not having the exact skill set required? It is also a good checkpoint for you to make sure you've identified the right person for the task or project: did you get the will and skill mix right?

You may have to show the person how to complete the task or project so they can continue without you, or partner them with another person who can train or show the delegate what to do.

Asking exploratory questions that encourage the delegate to think further will help; for example, try asking:

- *What have you considered so far?*
- *What do you think will make sense going forward?*

If they come to you with a question you believe they should already have an answer to, you could respond with:

- *This is a type of question I would think you might be able to work out for yourself. What have you done or tried so far?*

What if they don't know what support they need or want?

This might be the easiest to handle. If the delegate is unsure then offer to meet more often to start with and suggest you renegotiate support as you go. This way you are both being given the power to adjust as the task or project progresses and as needed.

Reverse Delegation

If you step in as soon as something goes wrong, you risk having to complete the task yourself, this is reverse delegation. Instead of simply stepping in and taking over, investigate (without blame) what went wrong and use this to help develop the delegate. Encourage the delegate to fix the situation and continue.

If you don't provide enough detail when delegating, for example, insufficient insight into how to navigate internal politics, or who to liaise with, or discuss who has completed the task prior, or even started the same project previously, you risk having to step in and pick up the pieces: this is also a form of reverse delegation. Your time spent planning using the templates provided in the downloads will help you to provide all the relevant information.

If you have delegated a task and its progress is slow, consider if you have provided positive reinforcement regarding the work done to date and you've expressed your confidence in the delegate's ability to complete the work. Without some acknowledgment of your confidence in them and appreciation for what has been done, the work might be left unfinished, leaving it for you to pick up the slack, especially as deadlines loom. This also is a form of reverse delegation.

If you end up doing the task or project you've delegated, it's important that you review your plan, the nine steps, and find where it was put into reverse and landed back on your desk. This is so you avoid it in the future.

In your Delegation Plan Template it will look like this:

SUPPORT:

How will you support the delegate? Consider what you believe is realistic support and discuss this with the delegate to come to an agreement of the level and type of support. This can be reviewed and changed as the delegation process continues.

POSSIBLE ROADBLOCKS:

What will hinder the success of this project? Identify as many roadblocks and objections to success as you can think of and note down your ideas to resolve them. This segment of the plan can be completed in conversation with the delegate however taking the time to think through problems and solutions helps you be more prepared for delegating and be more confident and feel in control.

You can find your complete Delegation Plan Template at
https://www.sallyfoleylewis.com/delegate-book-downloads/

6. Your Process: How - Agreed Tracking

Agreeing on how to track the progress of the task or project becomes easier to establish once you have a shared understanding of the outcome and an agreed approach to support.

In some instances, the tracking might simply be to let you know that the task is completed. In other instances, the tracking might include multiple levels of authority to sign off on different stages (or milestones). Discuss tracking even if it seems obvious, it's never safe to assume tracking is obvious.

By agreeing on the task or project tracking, you can confidently notice work that may be inaccurate or unacceptable before too long. It's easier and cheaper to fix a small mess now than a big mess later.

In your Delegation Plan Template it will look like this:

DEADLINES AND MILESTONES:

When must this whole task or project be completed? What milestones do you think need to be met for progress: these need to be agreed with the delegate but it helps for you to have considered these in the planning.

What are the consequences for an incomplete task or project? Linked to the purpose or the 'why' of the project, it might help to also understand what it means to the delegate, clients or customers, team and organisation if the task or project fails. This is NOT about creating a threat, it's about ensuring greater clarity of the task importance.

You can find your complete Delegation Plan Template at
https://www.sallyfoleylewis.com/delegate-book-downloads/

AFTER DELEGATING

7. Your Task: What - Lessons

Work is busy! Some days it can feel impossible to stop and think, however reflection is essential for learning and improving. What did delegating this task or project to that delegate teach you? Reflect on this question prior to asking the delegate what they learned from doing the task or project.

Better still, break your reflections down a little further, using this simple assessment. It will help you identify where you can improve your future delegating. You can complete the following assessment on your own or with the delegate. You can do it separately and then compare scores. Plotting along a scale from one (needs significant improvement) to five (done well), you will be able to see the areas for learning and the areas for the next step of acknowledging:

1. TASK IDENTIFICATION:

Unknown				Known
1	2	3	4	5

Why did you give that score:

2. WILL VERSUS SKILL:

Miss				Match
1	2	3	4	5

Why did you give that score:

3. PLAN:

Chaos				Course
1	2	3	4	5

Why did you give that score:

4. AGREED OUTCOME:

Confusion				Criteria
1	2	3	4	5

Why did you give that score:

5. AGREED SUPPORT:

Micromanage				Mentor
1	2	3	4	5

Why did you give that score:

6. AGREED TRACKING:

Mess				Milestones
1	2	3	4	5

Why did you give that score:

7. LESSONS:

Uninformed				Informed
1	2	3	4	5

Why did you give that score:

8. ACKNOWLEDGEMENTS:

Pass Over				Praise
1	2	3	4	5

Why did you give that score:

9. IMPROVED PLANNING:

Unproductive				Productive
1	2	3	4	5

Why did you give that score:

In your Delegation Plan Template it will look like this:

LESSONS:

What has been learned from this delegation?

Use the more in depth Delegation Lessons Assessment Form to unpack this segment in more detail.

You can find your complete Delegation Plan Template and Delegation Lessons Assessment Form at **https://www.sallyfoleylewis.com/delegate-book-downloads/**

8. Your People: Who - Acknowledgements

According to a study reported in the Harvard Business Review[14], 37% of the managers who took a self-assessment conceded that they don't give positive reinforcement. The results showed that managers believed their role was to correct direct reports if they make a mistake but to provide any praise was optional. The study extended to a 360-degree feedback survey and raters who thought a person was effective in giving feedback were most influenced by the leader's comfort and willingness to give positive reinforcement.

Giving praise for work done well ensures that the delegate feels valued and will be more inclined to accept more delegating opportunities in the future. Furthermore, others will notice and may step up their performance so delegation opportunities start to come their way too.

If the journey to completing the task or project was marred with all manner of challenges, even if the outcome didn't reach the expected, if

---

[14] https://hbr.org/2017/05/why-do-so-many-managers-avoid-giving-praise

the delegate gave all they had, then acknowledge their effort. Chances are, if the outcome fell short of expectations, the delegate will be just as disappointed as you will be, so acknowledging effort will help the delegate to want to improve, remedy and step up to future delegations.

Genuine and specific praise or acknowledgment is all that is required. Not everyone wants to be praised publicly so be mindful of how people like to receive feedback. You can learn more about feedback in *Successful Feedback: How Leaders Can Increase Performance, Motivate, and Engage Their Team*[15].

In your Delegation Plan Template it will look like this:

ACKNOWLEDGEMENTS:

How does the delegate like to be acknowledged? What do you need to acknowledge from this task or project? What did you think the delegate did well? Be specific.

You can find your complete Delegation Plan Template at
https://www.sallyfoleylewis.com/delegate-book-downloads/

9. Your Process: How - Improved Planning

Now that this task or project is completed, what needs to be included, excluded, fast-tracked, slowed down next time this task or project needs to be delegated?

As a means of continuous improvement, allocate some time, even if

[15] https://www.sallyfoleylewis.com/books/successful-feedback/

only a few minutes, to reflect on your entire delegating process so that your planning continues to improve.

One of the easiest ways to make sure you continue to get better and more confident in your delegating is to use the four-question reflections framework. You can work through these on your own, with the delegate, or complete separately and then compare answers.

MANAGER	DELEGATE
1. **Start:** What can I start doing more of to make delegating better?	1. **Start:** What can I start doing now that I have completed this task or project?
2. **Stop:** What do I need to stop doing in order to make delegating more effective?	2. **Stop:** What do I need to stop doing to make sure future delegations opportunities goes well?
3. **Continue:** What worked well and needs to be continued so I keep delegating successfully?	3. **Continue:** Now that this task or project is done, what needs to be continued in order to be productive or useful for me, the team and the company?
4. **Change:** What needs to be changed so that delegating is easier, smoother and more productive?	4. **Change:** What do I need to change in order to improve my way of handling and completing delegation opportunities?

In your Delegation Plan Template it will look like this:

IMPROVED PLANNING:

Without reflection there's no point trying to be a better delegator. What will you start, stop, change and continue next time you delegate?

You can find your complete Delegation Plan Template at **https://www.sallyfoleylewis.com/delegate-book-downloads/**

For everything we don't like to do, there's someone out there who's really good, wants to do it and will enjoy it.

JOSH KAUFMAN
AMERICAN SOUL SINGER & SINGER-SONGWRITER

CHAPTER 15

PUTTING IT ALL BACK TOGETHER

Now that you've worked through all nine steps methodically, it's time to put them all back together to give a complete picture of successful delegation.

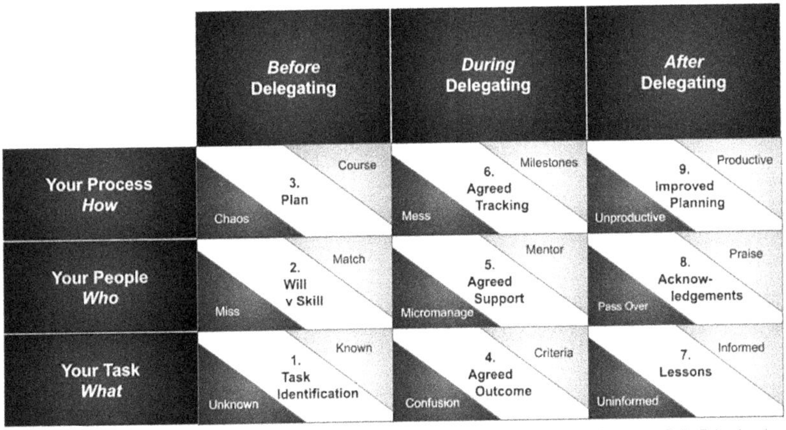

In summary:

Before Delegating:

1. **Task Identification:** detail what you know and investigate what you need to know.
2. **Will versus Skill:** match up relevant skills and willingness to do the task. What development opportunities are present for your team members?
3. **Plan:** create a course of action in order to avoid chaos.

During Delegating:

4. **Agreed Outcomes:** set and agree criteria so that there's no confusion.
5. **Agreed Support:** with a mutually agreed level and process of support, you can be a mentor and avoid micromanaging.
6. **Agreed Tracking:** Reaching known and agreed milestones, you both avoid a big mess.

After Delegating:

7. **Lessons:** How can this delegation keep you informed and even more ready for the next time?
8. **Acknowledgements:** Praise where praise is due because no one wants to feel unvalued or passed over.
9. **Improved Planning:** Delegating successfully means being more productive.

Now, it's over to you!

I have used this framework with team members, outsourced services, and trained this framework for years helping managers to be confident, successful delegators. It works. I'd love to hear from you once you've implemented these nine steps, let me know how you get on, you can reach me at *sally@sallyfoleylewis.com.*

It's your time to be a happy, productive leader and discerning delegator!

DELEGATE DOWNLOADS

Here are all the downloadable resources you need for your delegating success. You can download:

1. Barriers and Fears Tip Sheet
2. Delegation Decision Poster
3. Nine Steps Poster
4. Delegation Plan
5. Delegation Lessons

You can find your Delegation Plan Template at **https://www.sallyfoleylewis.com/delegate-book-downloads/**

Work with Sally

Over the last 20 years, I have worked with thousands of managers who work in a wide range of industries across many countries. I love to skill and support managers to be confident and productive. Through speaking, coaching and training I have found managers fall into three broad categories:

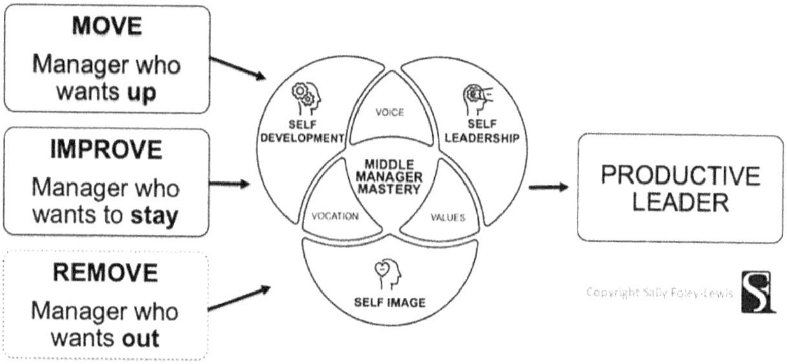

The manager on the move is ambitious and eager to climb the career ladder. Being able to implement a leadership development program for this manager helps keep the right person in the organisation longer and as such, the organisation gets a significant return on their investment.

Next is the manager who loves their role and simply wants to keep improving their leadership skills so they can continue to be an effective and productive leader of their team.

The manager who has discovered that being a manager is not suited to them means looking for ways to remove them or for them to remove themselves. People who step into management may have done so because it seemed that it was the obvious next step; maybe this is the only way the organisation could recognise great performance, or maybe there was pressure to earn more or to achieve a certain level of status. Helping managers move into roles they enjoy means creating the right environment for improved productivity. When a manager is disengaged and struggling because they've discovered they hate being a manager, their performance will eventually have an effect on the team and the bottom line. The organisation that can help this manager move with dignity and respect intact is an organisation that will earn loyalty and productivity, whether that person remains in the organisation or exits.

Mastering middle management is about creating productive leaders no matter what their actual role might be or might become.

I speak, train and coach middle management mastery, self-leadership and productive leadership. I do this through conference and meeting presentations, group and one-on-one coaching and mentoring, and short and in-depth development programs for managers. The focus is on helping managers who want to build their skills and confidence so they can lead their teams more confidently and effectively - by delegating appropriately, leading difficult conversations with confidence, and giving feedback in ways that affect positive change.

To find out more about Sally and her programs, go to www.sallyfoleylewis.com or let's book a time to chat: sally@sallyfoleylewis.com.

Subscribe to receive www.sallyfoleylewis.com

- Chapter One of Sally's book The Productive Leader
- A copy of The Productive Leader Whitepaper
- The Management Success Skills eBook
- Weekly Flow Notes
- Early release notice of events, programs, and free resources

Connect with Sally

LINKEDIN

https://www.linkedin.com/in/sallyfoleylewis/

FACEBOOK

https://www.facebook.com/PeopleAndProductivity/

YOUTUBE

http://www.youtube.com/c/SallyFoleyLewis

TWITTER

https://twitter.com/SallyFoleyLewis

INSTAGRAM

https://www.instagram.com/sallyfl/

Management Success Cards

- 65 colour coded self-coaching cards
- 12 essential management skills

https://www.sallyfoleylewis.com/books/management-success-cards/

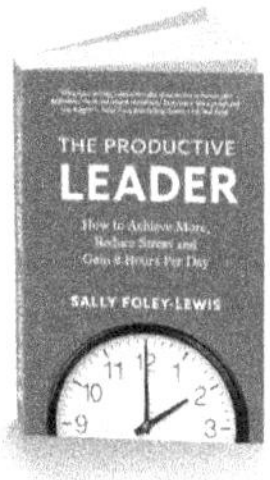

The Productive Leader

- How to achieve more, reduce stress and gain 2 hours per day

GRAB YOUR COPY

https://www.sallyfoleylewis.com/books/the-productive-leader/

Successful Feedback

GRAB YOUR COPY

- How leaders can increase performance, motivate and engage their team.

https://www.sallyfoleylewis.com/books/successful-feedback

Book Club for Professional Development - BCforPD™

- Read with accountability; read for professional and personal development; and grow your network and connections.

https://www.sallyfoleylewis.com/bc-for-pd/

PRAISE FOR *Sally's Work*

Sally delivered an engaging and practical session to the lawyers participating in the Queensland Law Society Open Day. They left with tips to take back and use right away. Time management does not have to be a dirty word!

DR. RACHEL BAIRD, GENERAL MANAGER

What a fantastic session at our conference! Sally shared examples and information that were relatable, equipping us with effective productivity strategies and reminded us of good habits we may have let slide. From GM and through the entire group, everyone has learned new tools and the buzz following the event indicates people are actually implementing them. Productive times (as a result of the personal graphs), chunking and email etiquette are only a few of the solutions in practice following the session. Sally's information, tools, energy, and interaction meant it was the best session of the conference!

ABBY FIELDS, GENERAL MANAGER

Couldn't recommend Sally highly enough. Sally took our after- lunch session of our National conference and got the group really going. She was engaging, developed relationships with individuals within the group, and even more impressively arrived early to watch our keynote speaker to ensure some continuity in the presentations.

KIARNI MORGANS, TEAM LEAD

Sally is the best! I was lucky to work with her on the Productive Leader Seminar on Nov 18,18th 2018 in Kuwait. One of the most cooperative and professional speakers I have worked with. Not only is she engaging, knowledgeable, and interactive during the seminar, but also she is a smooth communicator, understanding, and modest when dealing with others. She was very present and responsive from the first contact and contributed to making a very successful event with very high clients' feedback. I am glad I had the opportunity to work with her and will never hesitate to work with her again whenever there's an opportunity.

ABDUL-QUOM ALI, EVENTS, AND PRODUCT MANAGER

I had the pleasure of attending Sally's Boost Your Productivity Workshop and a follow up one-one session. I found Sally who then helped me understand the important elements of my role to give me focus, change my schedule and get the most out of my 'peaks', to allow me to improve my productivity at work, my staff and my life in general. Sally delivers her sessions with energy, humour, well-founded experience, and memorable anecdotes. I walked away feeling energised, and ready to take on my new role with a plan and enthusiasm.

JENNIFER TORRENS, STRATEGIC PLANNER

We have just finished a 3-month program working with Sally, and her approach to our team was refreshing and genuine. She allowed us to see a bit of the 'real' Sally, and challenged us in ways we needed to be challenged as a team. I have no doubt we will continue to work together with a strong team, moving into the future.

EMMA RHOADES, DEVELOPMENT COACH

I had the pleasure of attending Sally's session at the EAN Conference in Melbourne. Sally is personable, knowledgeable, and extremely engaging (not to mention very funny!). Sally has a real knack for getting people in the room to focus and pay attention. I am not a fan of audience participation but I would've done whatever she asked of me. I couldn't recommend her enough.

NICK GINSBURG, EA, AND FOUNDER OF HIGHER EDUCATION ASSISTANTS

You can see more recommendations and testimonials on Sally's LinkedIn profile and website.

www.ingramcontent.com/pod-product-compliance
Lightning Source LLC
Chambersburg PA
CBHW071425210326
41597CB00020B/3652
9780987418661